Guiding Those Left Behind
In Michigan
2nd Edition

LEGAL AND PRACTICAL THINGS
YOU NEED TO DO
TO SETTLE AN ESTATE IN MICHIGAN

and

HOW TO ARRANGE YOUR OWN AFFAIRS
TO PRESERVE YOUR ASSETS
AND PROVIDE FOR YOUR FAMILY

By AMELIA E. POHL, ESQ.

with Michigan attorney
CHRISTOPHER T. HAENICKE

 EAGLE PUBLISHING COMPANY OF BOCA

The purpose of this book is to provide the reader with an accurate
and informative overview of the subject but laws change frequently
and are subject to different interpretations as courts rule on the
meaning or effect of a law. This book is sold with the
understanding that neither the publisher nor the authors are
engaging in, nor rendering legal, medical, psychiatric,
accounting, financial planning, or any other professional service.
If you need legal, accounting, financial planning, medical,
psychiatric or other expert advice, then you should seek the
services of a licensed professional.

WEB SITES: Web sites appear throughout the book. These Web
sites are offered for the convenience of the reader only.
Publication of these Web site addresses is not an endorsement
by the authors, editors or publishers of this book.

This book is intended for use by the consumer for his or her own
benefit. If you use this book to counsel someone about the law,
accounting or medicine, then that may be considered an
unauthorized and illegal practice.

EAGLE PUBLISHING COMPANY OF BOCA
4199 N. Dixie Highway, #2
Boca Raton, FL   33431
E-mail   info@eaglepublishing.com

Printed in the United States of America
ISBN 1-892407-18-3
Library of Congress Card Catalog Number 00-190358

About the Author

Before becoming an attorney in 1985, AMELIA E. POHL taught mathematics on both the high school and college level. During her tenure as Associate Professor of Mathematics at Prince George's Community College in Maryland, she wrote several books including *Probability: A Set Theory Approach*, *Principals of Counting* and *Common Stock Sense*.

During her practice of law Attorney Pohl observed that many people want to reduce the high cost of legal fees by performing or assisting with their own legal transactions. Attorney Pohl found that, with a bit of guidance, people are able to perform many legal transactions for themselves. Attorney Pohl utilizes her background as teacher, author and attorney to provide that "bit of guidance" to the general public in the form of self-help legal books that she has written. Attorney Pohl is currently "translating" this book for the remaining 49 states:

Guiding Those Left Behind In Alabama,
Guiding Those Left Behind In Connecticut, etc.

Consulting Michigan Attorney

Christopher T. Haenicke is an attorney with the law firm of LEWISALLEN, P.C., in Kalamazoo, Michigan. Mr. Haenicke counsel clients in the areas of estate planning, elder law, and business law. His clients include individuals, limited liability companies, partnerships, and corporations (both for profit and non-profit).

Mr. Haenicke received his undergraduate degree from The Ohio State University. He graduated from the University of Cincinnati College of Law, and A member if the State Bar of Michigan, Mr. Haenicke is admitted to practice before all state and federal courts in Michigan.

Mr. Haenicke is very active in numerous charitable and nonprofit organizations in his community. He is president of the Board of Trustees of Guardian, Inc., which serves as guardian, conservator, and representative payee for protected individuals in the counties of Calhoun and Kalamazoo. Mr. Haenicke has served as secretary of the Kalamazoo County Bar Association, and is currently a member of its Board of Directors. He is also a member of the Executive Committee of the Kalamazoo County Republican Party, and has been appointed by the President of the United States to serve on the Selective Service Local Board for the State of Michigan.

ABOUT LEWISALLEN, P.C.
LEWISALLEN, P.C., is engaged in the general practice of law. The firm has nine attorneys with a wide diversity of backgrounds and numerous areas of legal expertise. Its attorney and paralegal staff have practiced together for more than 14 years. Highly respected by their peers, members of the firm have been elected to the presidencies of the State Bar of Michigan and local Bar Associations, and are well known in their community, not only for their professional competence but also for their civic leadership.

ACKNOWLEDGMENT

When someone dies, the family attorney is often among the first to be called. Family members have questions about whether probate is necessary, who to notify, how to get possession of the assets, etc. Over the years, as we practiced in the field of Elder Law, we noticed that the questions raised were much the same family to family. We both agreed that a book answering such questions would be of service to the general public.

We also observed, that those who had experience in settling the estate of a loved one had an understanding of the process, and were better able to make decisions about their own estate plan. We decided to combine the two topics: Settling An Estate and Estate Planning into a single book *Guiding Those Left Behind*.

We wish to thank all of the clients, whom we have had the honor and pleasure to serve, for providing us with the impetus to produce this book.

SPECIAL THANKS FROM AMELIA E. POHL

I wish to thank my brothers Paul and Fred Adinolfi, my daughters Louise Lucas and Margo Bosche, and my husband J. William Pohl. Working on this series of books was just that much easier because of the support given to me by all the members of my family.

SPECIAL THANKS FROM CHRISTOPHER T. HAENICKE

My participation in this book would not have been possible but for the support and encouragement I received from my family and my partners at LewisAllen, P.C. I would also like to give a special thanks to attorney John A. Scott of Traverse City, Michigan, who introduced me to Amelia E. Pohl.

The Organization of the Book

If you are going to GUIDE THOSE LEFT BEHIND, you need to know what is involved in settling an estate in Michigan, so we begin the book explaining that process. The first six chapters explain:

1. How to tend to the funeral and burial
2. What agencies need to be notified of the death
3. How to locate the decedent's property
4. What bills need (and do not need) to be paid.
5. Determining who are the beneficiaries
6. Getting the decedent's property to the proper beneficiary

We devoted a chapter to each of these 6 steps; and for those who are in the process of settling an estate, we placed a CHECK LIST at the end of Chapter 6 to assist in remembering things that need to be done.

Once you read Chapters 1 through 6 you will be able to identify those problems that can occur when someone dies. Using those Chapters as a base, the rest of the book explains how to set up your own estate plan so that your family is not burdened by similar problems.

GLOSSARY

This book is designed for the average reader. Legal terminology has been kept to a minimum. There is a glossary at the end of the book in the event you come across a legal term that is not familiar to you.

FICTITIOUS NAMES AND EVENTS

The examples in this book are based loosely on actual events; however, all names are fictitious; and the events, as portrayed, are fictitious.

Guiding Those Left Behind In Michigan

CONTENTS

About The Book

We tried to make this book as comprehensive as possible so there are specialized sections of the book that do not apply to the general population and may not be of interest to you. The following GUIDE POSTS appear throughout the book. You can read the section if the situation applies to you or skip the section if it doesn't.

GUIDE POSTS

The SPOUSE POST means that the information provided is specifically for the spouse of the decedent. If the decedent was single, then skip this section.

The CALL-A-LAWYER POST alerts you to a situation that may require the assistance of an attorney. See page xii for information about how to find a lawyer.

The CAUTION POST alerts you to a potential problem. It is followed by a suggestion about how to avoid the problem.

The SPECIAL SITUATION POST means that the information given in that paragraph applies to a particular event or situation; for example when the decedent dies a violent death. If the situation does not apply in your case then you can skip the section.

Reading the Law

Where applicable, we identified the state statute or federal statute that is the basis of the discussion. We did this as a reference, and also to encourage the general public to read the law as it is written. Prior to the Internet the only way you could look up the law was to physically take yourself to the local courthouse law library or the law section of a public library. Today all of the state and federal statutes are literally at your finger tips. They are just a mouse click away on the Internet. All you need to look up the law is the address of the Web site and the identifying number of the statute:

 MICHIGAN STATUTE WEB SITE
http://www.michiganlegislature.org/law

FEDERAL STATUTE WEB SITE
http://www4.law.cornell.edu/uscode

Michigan has compiled their laws into some 801 chapters. Each chapter is divided into sections. For example, to look up Michigan Compiled Law 52.205, you would look up Chapter 52, and then section 205 within that chapter. We will identify the law as (MCL 52.205).

If you come across a topic that is of importance to you, then you may find it both interesting and profitable to actually read the law as written.

When You Need A Lawyer

The purpose of the book is to give the reader a basic understanding of what needs to be done when someone dies, and to provide information about how a person can arrange his own affairs to avoid problems for his own family. It is not intended as a substitute for legal counsel or any other kind of professional advice. If you have any legal question, then you should to seek the counsel of an attorney. When looking for an attorney, consider three things: EXPERTISE, COST and PERSONALITY.

EXPERTISE

The state of Michigan does not have a program to certify that an attorney is specialized in a particular area of law. This being the case an attorney in Michigan may not represent to the public that he/she is a "specialist" in any given area of law. Attorneys are allowed to state that they concentrate on certain areas of law. Before employing an attorney for a job, ask how long he has practiced that type of law and what percentage of his practice is devoted to that type of law. Many counties have local Bar Associations with Lawyer Referral Services.

The Michigan State Bar Association has a Lawyer Referral Service. They can refer you to an attorney, in your area, for the type of legal service your seek. You can reach them at (800) 968-0738. The Michigan State Bar has a Web site with a list of Lawyer Referral Services throughout the state for attorneys who are licensed to practice in the state.

 MICHIGAN BAR WEB SITE
http://www.michbar.org

Of course, the best way to find an attorney is through personal referral. Ask your friends, family or business acquaintances if they ever used an attorney for the field of law that you seek and if so, whether they were pleased with the results. It is important to employ an attorney who is experienced in the area of law you seek. Your friend may have a wonderful Estate Planning attorney, but if you have suffered an injury, then you need a Personal Injury attorney.

Before employing an attorney for a job, ask how long he has practiced that type of law and what percentage of his practice is devoted to that type of law.

COST

In addition to the attorney's experience, it is important to check out what you can expect to pay in attorney's fees. When you call for an appointment ask what the attorney will charge for the initial consultation and the approximate cost for the service you seek. Ask whether there will be any additional costs such as filing fees, accounting fees, expert witness fees, etc.

If the least expensive attorney is out of your price range then you can call your local county Bar Association for the telephone number of the Legal Aid Society nearest you.

The American Bar Association has a directory of Michigan Legal Services Programs at the **General Public Resources** section of its Web site:

 AMERICAN BAR ASSOCIATION WEB SITE
http://www.abanet.org

PERSONALITY

Of equal importance to the attorney's experience and legal fees, is your relationship with the attorney. How easy was it to reach the attorney? Did you go through layers of receptionists and legal assistants before being allowed to speak to the attorney? Did the attorney promptly return your call? If you had difficulty reaching the attorney, then you can expect similar problems should you employ that attorney.

Did the attorney treat you with respect? Did the attorney treat you paternally with a "father knows best" attitude or did the attorney treat you as an intelligent person with the ability to understand the options available to you and the ability to make your own decision based on the information provided to you. Are you able to understand and easily communicate with the attorney? Is he/she speaking to you in plain English or is his/her explanation of the matter so full of legalese to be almost meaningless to you?

Do you find the attorney's personality to be pleasant or grating? Sometimes people rub each other the wrong way. It is like rubbing a cat the wrong way. Stroking a cat from head to tail is pleasing to the cat, but petting it in the opposite direction, no matter how well intended, causes friction. If the lawyer makes you feel annoyed or uncomfortable, then find another attorney.

It is worth the effort to take the time to interview as many attorneys as it takes to find one with the right expertise, fee schedule and personality for you.

The First Week 1

Dealing with the death of a close family member or friend is difficult. Not only do you need to deal with your own emotions, but often with those of your family and friends. Sometimes their sorrow is more painful to you, than what you are experiencing yourself.

In addition to the emotional impact of a death, there are many things that need to be done, from arranging the funeral and burial, to closing out the business affairs of the *decedent* (the person who died) and finally giving whatever property is left to the proper beneficiary.

The funeral and burial take only a few days. Wrapping up the affairs of the decedent may take considerably longer. This chapter explains what things you (the spouse or closest family member) need to do during the first week, beginning at the moment of death and continuing through the funeral.

 MALE GENDER USED

Rather than use "he/she" or "his/her" for simplicity
(and hoping not to offend anyone)
we will refer to the decedent and his
Personal Representative using the male gender.

References to other people will be in both genders.

AUTOPSIES

In today's high tech world of medicine, doctors are fairly certain of the cause of death, but if there is a question as to the cause of death, the doctor may ask whoever is taking responsibility for the burial (parent, surviving spouse, guardian, next of kin) to give written consent for the procedure (MCL 333.2855). The person giving authorization must agree to pay for the autopsy because the cost is not covered under most health insurance plans.

The cost of an autopsy can run anywhere from several hundred to well over three thousand dollars, but it is in the family's best interest to consent to the autopsy. The examination might reveal a genetic disorder, that could be treated if it later appears in another family member. Death from a car "accident" could have been a heart attack at the wheel. Perhaps the patient who died suddenly in a hospital was misdiagnosed. The nursing home resident could have died from negligence and not old age. Even if none of these are found, knowing the cause of death with certainty is better than not knowing.

That was the case with the family of a woman who was taken to the hospital complaining of stomach pains. The doctors thought she might be suffering from gallbladder disease but she died before they could effectively treat her. A doctor suggested that an autopsy be performed to determine the actual cause of death. The woman had three daughters, one of whom objected to the autopsy: "Why spend that kind of money? It won't bring Mom back."

The daughter's wishes were respected, however over the years as they aged and became ill with their own various ailments they would undergo physical examinations. As part of taking their medical history, doctors routinely asked "And what was the cause of your mother's death?"

None could answer the question.

This is not a dramatic story. No mysterious genetic disorder ever occurred in any of her daughters, nor in any of their children. But each daughter (including the one who objected) at some point in her life, was confronted with the nagging question "What did Mom die of?"

MANDATORY AUTOPSIES
When a person dies, a physician, or his authorized agent, must sign the death certificate stating the cause of death. If a person dies in a hospital, then there is someone present to sign the certificate. If a person dies at home from natural causes and he was examined by a physician within ten days of the death, then the physician can sign the death certificate and the funeral director can take possession of the body. In such case, there is no need to call 911. But if a person discovers a body of a person who was not under the care of a physician, or who died suddenly either from illness, accident, suicide or foul play, then the police must be summoned. The police will ask the County Medical Examiner to determine the cause of death. The Medical Examiner will have an autopsy performed whenever there is a suspicion that the death was not from natural causes or that the death was caused by a disease that poses a threat to the public health (MCL 52.205, 333.1033, 333.2844).

AUTOPSIES PERFORMED BY THE INSURANCE COMPANY
A company that issues a policy of disability insurance, including accident and sickness insurance in the state of Michigan is required to include a provision in their policy stating that the company has the right to perform an autopsy (MCL 500.3400, 500.3420). The cost of the autopsy is paid for by the insurance company, so they will not order an autopsy unless there is some important reason to do so.

ANATOMICAL GIFTS

If, before death, the decedent made an anatomical gift by signing a donor card, then hospital personnel or the donor's doctor needs to be made aware of the gift in quick proximity to the time of death — preferably before death.

GIFT AUTHORIZED BY THE FAMILY

Hospital personnel determine whether a mortally ill patient is a candidate for an organ donation. Early on in the donor program those over 65 were not considered as suitable candidates. Today, however, the condition of the organ, and not the age, is the determining factor.

The federal government has established regional Organ Procurement Organizations throughout the United States to coordinate the donor program. The Organ Procurement Organization for Michigan is the Transplantation Society of Michigan located at Ann Arbor. If it is decided that the patient is a candidate, the hospital will contact the Transplantation Society.

The Transplantation Society will determine whether the patient is a suitable donor. If they decide to request the gift and the candidate did not sign a donor card then someone in the family must give written permission. Someone who is specially trained will approach the family to request the donation.

Michigan statute states an order of priority for those who can give permission:

1st Spouse   2nd Adult son or daughter
3rd Either parent   4th An adult brother or sister
5th The guardian of the decedent at time of death
6th Anyone else who is authorized to dispose of the body

If permission is obtained from a family member and there are others in the same or a higher priority, then an effort must be made to contact those people and make them aware of the proposed gift. For example, if the sister of the decedent agrees to the gift (4th in priority) and the decedent had an adult child (2rd in priority), then the child needs to be made aware of the gift. If the child objects, then no gift can be made. Similarly, the statute prohibits the gift if the decedent ever expressed his opposition to a donation (MCL 333.10102).

AFTER THE DONATION

Once the donation is made the body is delivered to the funeral home and prepared for burial or cremation as directed by the family. The donation does not disfigure the body so there can be an open casket viewing if the family so wishes.

Some regional Organ Procurement Organizations have an aftercare program that includes a letter of condolence to the family and an expression of gratitude for the gift. For privacy reasons, the identity of the recipient of the gift is not disclosed, but on request from the family, the local Organ Procurement Organization will give the family basic demographic information about the donation, such as the age, sex, marital status, number of children and occupation of the recipient of the gift.

GIFT FOR EDUCATION OR RESEARCH

If the decedent signed a donor card indicating his wish to use his body for any purpose and he is not a candidate for an organ donation, then you can offer to release the body, for the purpose of education or research, to a school of medicine at a university, such as:

Wayne State Univ., School of Medicine   (313) 577-1188
Dept. of Anatomy; 549 E. Canfield Ave,
Detroit, MI 48201

Univ. of Michigan, Medical Center   (734) 764-4359
Dept. of Anatomy
3626 Medical Sciences, Bldg. II
Ann Arbor, MI 48109

Michigan State Univ., Dept of Anatomy   (517) 353-5398
East Free Hall, C-203
East Lansing, MI 48824

You will need to call the school to determine whether they will accept the body. Most schools will not accept bodies from those who have died from a contagious disease or from crushing injuries. If the donation is accepted, then the body should not be embalmed before it is transported. The school will pay for transporting the body to the school provided it is local to the area.

The study can take anywhere from two weeks to two years. At the end of the study the remains are cremated. The *cremains* (cremated remains) will be placed in a cemetery that is local to the university; or if the family wishes, the cremains will be delivered to the next of kin.

CAVEAT: It is a felony for anyone to purchase body parts in the state of Michigan (MCL 333.10204). It is not illegal to charge monies to prepare or transport bodies or body parts. Not-for profit and as well as for-profit companies have sprung up that are in the business of preparing and delivering body parts. These companies request donations from families (so they are not buying body parts). The company prepares the body tissue or other parts of the body, and then distributes the parts throughout the United States to physicians, hospitals, research centers, etc. In many cases the monies charged for preparation and transportation include a sizable profit.

LEARN ABOUT THE COMPANY

If someone other than your local Organ Procurement Organization (The Transplantation Society of Michigan) approaches you to make a donation, then before making the donation you may want to learn about the company requesting the donation.

> What is the name of the company?
> Where are their main headquarters located?
> What is their primary business activity?
> What is the name and job description of the
> person making the request?

DETERMINE THE END USE OF THE DONATION

You may want to ask what they intend to do with the tissue or body part. If it is being used for research, then what type of research? Where is the research being conducted? If it will be used for transplantation, then what agency (doctor, hospital) will receive the donation and where is that agency located?

Once you have this information you can make an informed decision as to whether you wish to make the donation.

THE FUNERAL

Approximately ten percent of all deaths occur suddenly because of an accident, suicide, foul play or undetected illness . But most deaths occur after a lengthy illness with a common scenario being that of an aged person dying after being ill for several months. In such cases, family and friends are emotionally prepared for the happening. Expected or not, the first job is the disposition of the body.

THE PREARRANGED FUNERAL

Increasingly, people are arranging, in advance, for their own funeral and burial. This makes it easier on the family both financially and emotionally. All the decisions have been made and there is no guessing what the decedent would have wanted.

If the decedent made provision for his burial, then you should come across a burial certificate, or perhaps a deed to a burial space. If he made provision for his funeral, then you should find a Preneed funeral contract. You need to read the contract to determine what provisions were made. If the contract was paid on a basis, then you need to determine whether it is paid in full. You also need to determine whether the contract was a fixed price agreement or whether there could be additional charges.

If you cannot locate the contract, but you know the decedent made provision for his funeral, then call the funeral home and ask them to send you a copy of the contract. If you believe the decedent purchased a funeral plan but you do not know the name of the funeral home, then call the local funeral homes. Many local funeral homes are owned by national firms with computer capacity to identify people who have purchased a contract in any of their many locations.

Once you have possession of the contract, take it with you to the funeral home and go over the terms of the contract with the funeral director. Inquire whether there is any charge that is not included in the contract.

MAKING FUNERAL ARRANGEMENTS

If the decedent died unexpectedly or without having made any prior funeral arrangements then your first job is to choose a funeral director and make arrangements for the funeral or cremation. Most people choose the nearest or most conveniently located funeral home without comparison shopping. However prices for these services can vary significantly from funeral home to funeral home. Savings can be had if you take the time to make a few phone calls.

Receiving price quotes by telephone is your right under Federal law. Federal Trade Commission ("FTC") Rule 453.2 (b) (1) requires a funeral director to give an accurate telephone quote of the prices of his goods and services. Funeral homes are listed in the telephone directory under FUNERAL DIRECTORS. If you live in a small town, there may be only one or two listings. If such is the case, then check out some funeral homes in the next largest city.

Funeral Directors usually provide the following services:
➢ arrange for the transportation of the body
    to the funeral home and then to the burial site
➢ obtain burial transit permits
➢ arrange for the embalming or cremation of the body
➢ arrange funeral and memorial services
    and the viewing of the body
➢ obtain information for the death certificate
➢ order copies of the death certificate for the family
➢ have memorial cards printed.

To compare prices you will need to determine:

✧ what is included in the price of a basic funeral plan

✧ whether you can expect any additional cost.

If the decedent did not own a burial space, then that cost must be included when making funeral arrangements.

It may be necessary to have the body embalmed if you are going to have a viewing. Embalming is not necessary if you order a direct cremation or an immediate burial without a viewing. Federal Trade Commission Rule 453.5 prohibits the funeral home from charging an embalming fee unless you order the service.

PURCHASING THE CASKET

When comparison-shopping, you will find that the single most expensive item to be a casket. When selecting a casket you need to be aware that there may be a considerable mark-up in the price quoted by the funeral director. You do not need to go "sole source" when purchasing the casket. If you feel that the price quoted by the funeral director is too high, you can purchase the casket elsewhere and have it delivered to the funeral home to be used instead of the one offered by the funeral director. Federal regulations require a funeral home to accept a casket that is purchased elsewhere.

The funeral director must provide you with a written price list at the beginning of your discussion of funeral arrangements. If the price list given to you by the funeral home states that the price of their casket includes a specific dollar amount for basic services, and you do not purchase the casket from the funeral home, then the funeral director is allowed to add that specific dollar amount to the charge for his basic services. He is not allowed to charge a handling fee for accepting a casket that is purchased elsewhere (FTC Rule 453.2, 453.4).

Of course the problem with purchasing a casket is that most of us have no idea what to pay. Caskets are not usually displayed for sale in a shopping mall, so how do you determine the going price? The answer is the Internet. You can learn all about the cost of any item, even a casket, by using your search engine to find a retail casket sales dealer. If you are not computer literate, you can locate the nearest retail casket sales outlet by looking in the yellow pages under CASKETS. You may need to look in the telephone directory for the nearest large city to find a listing. By making a call to a retail casket sales dealer, you will become knowledgeable in the price range of caskets. You can then decide what is a reasonable price for the product you seek.

The best time to do your comparison shopping, is before you go to the funeral home to arrange for the funeral. Once you have determined what you should pay for the casket, it is only fair to give the funeral director the opportunity to meet that price. If you cannot reach a meeting of the minds, then you can always order the casket from the retail sales dealer and have it delivered to the funeral home.

ON-LINE FUNERAL SERVICES

The Internet is changing the way the world does business, and the funeral industry is no exception. A growing number of mortuaries are offering live Webcasts of funerals and wakes for those who are unable to pay their respects in person.

There are Web sites such as ObitDetails.com where you can post an obituary. There are on-line memorial chat rooms as well as online eulogies and testimonials. There is even a Web site that offers a posthumous e-mail service which allows people to leave final messages for friends and relatives.

THE CREMATION

Increasingly people are opting for cremation. The reasons for choosing cremation are varied, but for the majority, it is a matter of finances. The cost of cremation is approximately one-sixth that of an ordinary funeral and burial. A major saving is the cost of the casket. No casket is necessary for the cremation and Federal law prohibits a Funeral Director from saying that a casket is required for a direct cremation (FTC Rule 453.3 (b)ii). You may need a suitable container to deliver the body to the crematory. After the cremation, you will need an urn for the ashes.

If you are having a memorial service in a place of worship and no viewing of the body before the cremation, then consider contracting with a facility that does cremations only. Look in the telephone book CREMATION SERVICES. You will also see cremation "societies" in the telephone book. Some are for-profit and others non-profit. You can also find advertisements for cremation services on the Internet.

THE OVERWEIGHT DECEDENT
If the decedent weighs more than 300 pounds, then you need to check to see if the Cremation service has facilities large enough to handle the body. If you cannot locate a crematory that can accommodate the body, then you will need to make burial arrangements.

THE DECEDENT WITH A PACEMAKER
Cremating a body with a pacemaker or any radiation producing devise can cause damage to the cremation chamber or to the person performing the cremation. If the decedent was wearing such electronic aid, then you need to investigate the cost of having it removed prior to the cremation. The Cremation service may be able help you to arrange for the removal of the device.

DISPOSING OF THE ASHES

The decedent's cremains can be placed in a cemetery. Many cemeteries have a separate building called a **columbarium**, which is especially designed to store urns. If not, then the cremains can be placed in a cemetery plot. Some cemeteries allow the cremains of a family member to be placed in an occupied family plot. Similarly, some cemeteries will allow the cremains to be place in the space in a mausoleum that is currently occupied by a member of the decedent's family. If it is your desire to have the cremains placed in an occupied mausoleum or family plot, then you need to call the cemetery and ask them to explain their policy as it relates to the burial of urns in occupied sites.

If the cremains are to be placed in a cemetery, then you need to obtain a suitable urn for the burial. You can purchase the urn from the Funeral Director or Crematory Service Director. Urns cost much less than caskets, but they can cost several hundred dollars. You may wish to do some comparison shopping by calling a retail sales casket dealer.

The decedent may have expressed a desire that his ashes be spread out to sea. The Funeral Director or Cremation Service Director can assist you with such arrangements.

```
┌──────────────┐
│ Special      ╲
│ Situation    ╱    THE OUT OF STATE BURIAL
└──────────────┘
```

If the decedent is to be buried in another state, then the body will need to be transported to that state. Most funeral homes belong to a national network of funeral homes, and the out-of-state Funeral Director has the means to make local arrangements to ship the body. Contact the out-of-state Funeral Director and have him/her make arrangement with the airline for the transportation of the body.

If services are to be held in Michigan and in another state, then contact the local funeral director and he will make arrangements with the out-of-state funeral home for the transportation of the body.

If the body has been cremated, then you can transport the cremains yourself, either by carrying the ashes as part of your luggage or by arranging with the airline to transport the ashes as cargo. Have a certified copy of the death certificate available in the event that you need to identify the remains of the decedent. Call the airline before departure and ask whether they have any special regulation or procedure regarding the transportation of human ashes.

| SPOUSE | THE MILITARY BURIAL

Subject to availability of burial spaces, an honorably discharged veteran and/or his unmarried minor or handicapped child and/or his un-remarried spouse may be buried in a national military cemetery. Some cemeteries have room only for cremated remains or for the casketed remains of a family member of someone who is currently buried in that cemetery, so you need to call for space availability.

There is one national military cemetery in Michigan and they currently have space available:

Fort Custer National Cemetery
15501 Dickman Road
Augusta, MI   49012
Telephone: (616) 731-4164

The Department of the Army is in charge of the Arlington National Cemetery. If you wish to have an eligible deceased veteran buried in the Arlington National Cemetery, then call them at (703) 695-3250 or write to them at:

Arlington National Cemetery
Interment Service Branch
Arlington, VA 22211

THE COST OF A MILITARY BURIAL

Burial space in a National Cemetery is free of charge. Cemetery employees will open and close the grave and mark it with headstone or grave marker without cost to the family. The local Veteran's Administration ("VA") will provide the family with a memorial flag. The family needs to make funeral arrangements with a funeral firm and have them transport the remains to the cemetery.

Regardless of where an honorably discharged veteran, is buried, allowances may be available for the plot, and burial and grave marker expenses. The amount varies depending on factors such as whether the veteran died because of a service related injury. The VA will not reimburse any burial or funeral expense for the spouse of a veteran.

For information about reimbursement of funeral and burial expenses you can call the VA at (800) 827-1000.

The Department of Veteran's Affairs has a Web site with information on the following topics:

➤ National and Military Cemeteries
➤ Burial, Headstones and Markers
➤ State Cemetery Grants Program
➤ Obtaining Military Records
➤ Locating Veterans

VA CEMETERY WEB SITE
http://www.cem.va.gov

SPOUSE ➤ BENEFITS FOR SPOUSE OF DECEDENT VETERAN

The surviving spouse of an honorably discharged veteran should contact the Veteran's Administration to determine whether he/she is eligible for any benefits. For example, if the decedent had minor or disabled children, his spouse may also be eligible for a monthly benefit of Dependency and Indemnity Compensation ("DIC"). If the Veteran's surviving spouse receives nursing home care under Medicaid, then the spouse might be eligible for monthly payments from the VA.

Whether a surviving spouse is eligible for any of these benefits depends on many factors including whether the decedent was serving on active duty, whether his death was service related, and the surviving spouse's assets and income. DIC benefits are discontinued should the surviving spouse remarry; however, a recent change in the law permits payments to be resumed, should the subsequent marriage end because of death or divorce.

For information about whether the surviving spouse is eligible for any benefit related to the decedent's military service call the VA at (800) 827-1000. You can receive a printed statement of public policy: VA Pamphlet 051-000-00217-2 FEDERAL BENEFITS FOR VETERANS AND DEPENDENTS by sending a check in the amount of $5 to
THE SUPERINTENDENT OF DOCUMENTS
P.O. Box 371954
Pittsburgh, PA 15250-7954
Information is also available at the VA Web site:

VA WEB SITE
http://www.va.gov

 **☎ LAWYER** THE VIOLENT DEATH

If the decedent died a violent death or under circumstances in which foul play is suspected, the Medical Examiner will take possession of the body (MCL 52.205). The body will not be released to the funeral director until the examination of the body is complete. In the interim, the family can proceed with arrangements for the funeral. The funeral director will contact the Medical Examiner to determine when he can pick up the body and proceed with the funeral.

If the decedent died because of an accident then it is important to contact a Personal Injury attorney to determine whether they have a case for wrongful death. If the accident was related to the decedent's job, the family may wish to consult with a Worker's Compensation attorney as well.

THE WRONGFUL DEATH
Should a person die because of a wrongful act of another person or company, then the decedent's next of kin have the right to be compensated for that loss. A Personal Representative will need to be appointed to sue on behalf of the decedent. If a settlement is offered, then the Probate court will need to approve settlement and to decide who will receive the proceeds of the settlement funds. (MCL 600.2922; 700.3924).

If the decedent died because of a criminal act and you are a family member, then you may wish to contact an attorney experienced in Criminal Law to learn of your rights as a family member.

| Special Situation | VICTIMS OF CRIME COMPENSATION PROGRAM |

If the decedent died because of a criminal act and you are a family member (spouse, child, parent, sibling, grandparent), then you may be eligible to receive compensation under the **VICTIMS OF CRIME ACT**. This program is funded jointly by the state and federal government. In Michigan, compensation can be awarded for reasonable funeral expenses (up to $2,000), grief counseling (up to $500), and for medical expenses, travel fees and other costs. Total compensation may not be greater than $15,000 (MCL 18.361, 780.752).

The Michigan Crime Victims Services Commission administers the program. You will need to file a claim within one year of the commission of the crime. The Crime Victims Services Commission will investigate your claim. The investigation may take several weeks to complete. If emergency funds are needed, the Commission can award up to $500. Any award of emergency funds will be deducted from the final award (MCL 18.359, 780.903).

To file a claim you can call the Commission at (517) 373-7373 or write to them:

CRIME VICTIMS SERVICES COMMISSION
320 S. Walnut Street
Lansing, MI   48913

There is more about the program on the Internet:

 U.S. OFFICE OF JUSTICE WEB SITE
http://www.ojp.usdoj.gov/ovc/

THE UNCLAIMED BODY

If an indigent person dies and the police know his identity, they will try to locate the family. If the identity of the decedent is unknown, then the County Medical Examiner will try to identify the body and notify his next of kin (MCL 52.205, 333.2653).

If the decedent was without funds for burial and his family unknown, or if known, unable or unwilling to arrange for burial, then the official in charge of the body will offer the body to the Director of the Department of Community Health. The Director will have the body assigned to the Anatomy Department of a hospital or educational institution for the purpose of instruction or study (MCL 333.2652).

If a person dies while at a facility that is maintained at public expense (correctional facility, city hospital, mental health facility, etc.), then the official in charge will make every effort to notify the family of the death. If body is unclaimed within 72 hours of the death, the person in possession of the body will offer the body to the Department of Community Health to be used for educational purposes (MCL 333.2653, 333.26324).

THE INDIGENT VETERAN
If the decedent was an honorably discharged veteran, then the family can arrange to have a Veteran's burial. If the police cannot locate the family of a deceased veteran, then the county will contact the VA and arrange for the burial.

> **Special
> Situation**

THE PROBLEM
FUNERAL OR BURIAL

The funeral and burial industry is well regulated by both state and federal government. Under Michigan law (MCL 338.1810) the following acts are subject to disciplinary action:

☒ Knowingly making a false statement on the death certificate

☒ Paying kick-backs to generate business or receiving money to recommend a cemetery mausoleum, or crematory

☒ Using profane, indecent or obscene language in the presence of a dead body or within hearing of the family.

☒ Using a casket that has been previously used to dispose of a body.

Funeral directors are licensed professionals so it is unusual to have a problem with the funeral or burial or cremation. If, however, you had a bad experience with any aspect of the funeral then you can file a complaint with the state licensing agency:

**Michigan Department of Consumer & Industry Services
Board of Examiners in Mortuary Science
P.O. Box 30018
Lansing, MI 48909
Telephone (519) 241-9252**

 **☎ LAWYER**

In addition to filing a complaint with the Board, you may wish to consult with an attorney who is experienced in litigation matters to learn of any other legal remedy that you may have.

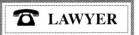**LAWYER**   THE MISSING BODY

Few things are more difficult to deal with than a missing person. The emotional turmoil created by the "not knowing" is often more difficult than the finality of death. The legal problems created by the disappearance are also more difficult than if the person simply died. It may take a two-part legal process to settle the estate — first appointing a someone, a *Conservator* to manage and protect the missing person's property while he is missing; and then a final Probate procedure if it determined that he is dead.

If the missing person was a disaster victim or in an accident and his remains cannot be found, then after 63 days have passed, any interested person (spouse, next of kin, beneficiary under the Will, creditor, etc.) can *petition* (ask) the Probate Court to have a hearing for the purpose determining the date and cause of death.

If a person is missing, without any known cause, then after 5 years, any interested person can ask the Court for an Order stating that the missing person is dead. Meanwhile, if there are matters that need attending (bills to be paid, children to be cared for, etc.), the Court can appoint a Conservator to handle the missing person's affairs until he is found or declared to be dead.

The Probate procedure can begin as soon as there is an Order establishing that the missing person is dead. It is not necessary to wait five years if at any time there is sufficient evidence for the Court to conclude that the missing person is dead (MCL 700.1207, 700.1208, 700.5401)

THE DEATH CERTIFICATE

It is the job of the Funeral Director or Cremation Service Director to provide information about the decedent to the Michigan Vital Records office. The office will prepare a death certificate based on that information. It is important that the information you give to the Funeral or Cremation Director is correct. It is also important that you check the form completed by the Funeral or Cremation Director to be sure names are correctly spelled and dates correctly written. Once the information is submitted to the Office of Vital Statistics, it will be difficult and time consuming to make a correction.

The Funeral or Cremation Director will order as many certified copies of the death certificate as you request. Most establishments require an original certified copy and not a photocopy so you need to order sufficient copies. The following is a list of institutions that may want a certified copy:

* Each insurance company that insured the decedent or his property (health insurance, life insurance, car insurance, etc.)
* Each financial institution in which the decedent had money invested (brokerage houses, banks)
* The decedent's pension fund
* Each credit card company used by the decedent
* The IRS
* The Social Security Administration
* The Register of Deeds in each county where the decedent owned real property
* If a Probate procedure is necessary, then the Clerk of the Probate Court

ORDERING COPIES OF THE DEATH CERTIFICATE

Some airlines and car rental companies offer a discount for short notice, emergency trips. If you have family flying in for the funeral, you may wish to order a few extra copies of the death certificate so that they can obtain an airline or car rental discount. If you wish to order certified copies of the death certificate at a later date, you can call the funeral director and ask him to do so or you can contact the Clerk in the county of the decedent's residence (MCL 333.2815). Not all counties carry Vital Records. You can check the Internet to see if you can order the death certificate from the county Clerk:

 MICHIGAN VITAL RECORDS
http://vitalrec.com/mi.html

You can order the death certificate from the state by writing to the **Michigan Department of Community Health**
c/o Vital Records
P.O. Box 30195
3423 N. Logan Street
Martin Luther King Jr. Blvd.
Lansing, MI   48914

You may save some time by first calling (517) 335-8666 and asking what information they require. The current charge is $13 for each search including one certified copy. Each additional copy costs $4. They accept checks or money order payable to the **STATE OF MICHIGAN.** If you need a death certificate quickly, you can fax your request to them at (517) 321-5884. They will mail the death certificate to you within two business days for an additional charge of $5. You will need to include your name, credit card number, expiration date and your signature within your faxed request. It is best to first call to determine what information they require.

About Probate

Once a person dies, all of the property he owns as of the date of his death is referred to as the *decedent's estate.* If the decedent owned property that was in his name only (not jointly or in trust for someone) then some sort of court procedure may be necessary to determine who is entitled to possession of the property. The name of the court procedure is *Probate.* The name of the court that conducts those procedures is the *Probate Court* (MCL 600.801, 700.1103, 700.1302)

The root of the word Probate is "to prove." It refers to the first job of the Probate Court, that is, to examine proof of whether the decedent left a valid Will. The second job of the Probate Court is to appoint someone, to be the decedent's *Personal Representative*, to wrap up the affairs of the decedent — to pay any outstanding bills and then to distribute what property is left to the beneficiaries.

If the decedent left a valid Will naming someone to be the Personal Representative, or Executor, of his estate, then the Court will appoint that person for the job. If the decedent died without a Will, the Court will appoint a Personal Representative to administer the estate. The documents issued by the Court that authorize the Personal Representative to act are called the *Letters of Authority.*

There are different ways to conduct a Probate procedure depending on the value of the property that being Probated, and whether the decedent owned real property at the time of his death. We will refer to the property that is distributed as part of a Probate procedure as the decedent's *Probate Estate* and the method of conducting a Probate procedure as the *Estate Administration*. Chapter 6 explains the different kinds of Estate Administration that are available in the state of Michigan.

But we are getting ahead of ourselves. First we need to determine whether a Probate procedure is necessary. To answer that question we need to know exactly what the decedent owned, so the next two chapters explain how to identify, and then locate, all of the decedent's assets.

Giving Notice Of The Death 2

Those closest to the decedent usually notify family members and close friends by telephone. The funeral director will arrange to have an obituary published in as many different newspapers as the family requests, but there is still the job of notifying the government and people who were doing business with the decedent. That task belongs to the person named as the Personal Representative, or Executor, of the decedent's Will. If the decedent died without a Will, then the spouse has the right to be appointed as Personal Representative. If there is no spouse, or if the spouse is unable or unwilling to serve, then anyone who has the right to inherit the decedent's property can be appointed (MCL 700.3203).

If no Probate procedure is necessary, the job of notifying people of the death and settling the decedent's affairs falls to his spouse; and in the absence of a spouse, to the decedent's next of kin. By *next of kin,* we mean those people who inherit the decedent's property according to the MICHIGAN INTESTATE SUCCESSION ACT. That law is explained in Chapter 5.

The person who has the job of settling the decedent's estate should begin to give notice as soon as is practicable after the death. Two government agencies that need to be notified are the Social Security Administration and the IRS. This chapter gives their telephone number and other agencies that need to be notified.

NOTIFYING SOCIAL SECURITY

Many Funeral Directors will, as part of their service package, notify the Social Security Administration of the death. You may wish to check to see that this has been done. You can do so by calling (800) 772-1213. If you are hearing impaired call (800) 325-0778 TTY. You will need to give the Social Security Administration the full legal name of the decedent as well as his social security number and date of birth.

 Special Situation

DECEDENT RECEIVING SOCIAL SECURITY CHECKS

If the decedent was receiving checks from Social Security, then you need to determine whether his last check needs to be returned to the Social Security Administration.

Each Social Security check is a payment for the prior month, provided that person lives for the entire prior month. If someone dies on the last day of the month, then you should not cash the check for that month. For example, if someone dies on July 31st, then you need to return the check that the agency mails out in August. If however, the decedent died on August 1st then the check sent in August need not be returned because that check is payment for the month of July.

If the Social Security check is electronically deposited into a bank account then notify the bank that the account holder died and notify the Social Security Administration as well. If the check needs to be returned, then the Social Security Administration will withdraw it electronically from the bank account. You will need to keep the account open until the funds are withdrawn.

SPOUSE/CHILD'S SOCIAL SECURITY BENEFITS

SPOUSE

If the decedent had sufficient work credits, the Social Security Administration will give the decedent's widow(er) or if unmarried, then the decedent's minor children, a one-time death benefit in the amount of $255.

SURVIVORS BENEFITS:

The spouse (or ex-spouse) of the decedent may be eligible for Survivors Benefits. Benefits vary depending on the amount of work credits earned by the decedent; whether the decedent had minor or disabled children; the spouse's age; how long they were married; etc. The minor child of the decedent may be eligible for benefits regardless of whether the child's father (the decedent) ever married the child's mother. Paternity can be established by any one of several methods including the father acknowledging his child in writing or verbally to members of his family. For more information you can call the Social Security Administration at (800) 772-1213.

SOCIAL SECURITY BENEFITS

A spouse or ex-spouse can collect social security benefits based on the decedent's work record. This value may be greater than the spouse now receives. It is important to make an appointment with your local Social Security office and determine whether you as the spouse (or ex-spouse) or parent of decedent's minor child are eligible for any Social Security or Survivor benefit. The Social Security Administration has a Web site from which you can down load publications that explain survivors benefits:

SOCIAL SECURITY WEB SITE
http://www.ssa.gov

DECEDENT WITH GOVERNMENT PENSION

If the decedent was a federal retiree and received a government pension then any check received after the date of death needs to be returned to the U.S. Treasury. If the check is direct deposited to a bank account, then call the financial institution and ask them to return the check. If the check is sent by mail then you need to return it to: **Director, Regional Finance Center**
U. S. Treasury Department
P.O. Box 7367
Chicago, IL 60680
Include a letter explaining the reason for the return of the check and stating the decedent's date of death.

$$$*   APPLY FOR BENEFITS   *$$$

Even though you notify the government of the death, they will not automatically give you benefits to which you may be entitled. You need to apply for those benefits by notifying the Office of Personnel Management ("OPM") of the death and requesting that they send you an application for survivor benefits. You can call them at (888) 767-6738 or you can write to:
THE OFFICE OF PERSONNEL MANAGEMENT
SERVICE AND RECORDS CENTER
BOYERS, PA 16017
You will find brochures and information about Survivor's Benefits at the OPM Web site:

OFFICE OF PERSONNEL MANAGEMENT WEB SITE
http://www.opm.gov
You can get assistance via E-mail at
retire@opm.gov

| Special Situation | DECEDENT WITH COMPANY PENSION OR ANNUITY |

In most cases, pension and annuity checks are payment for the prior month. If the decedent received his pension or annuity check before his death, then no monies need be returned. Pension checks and/or annuity checks received after the date of death may need to be returned to the company. You need to notify the company of the death to determine the status of the last check sent to the decedent.

Before notifying the company, locate the policy or pension statement that is the basis of the income. That document should tell whether there is a beneficiary of the pension or annuity funds now that the pensioner or annuitant is dead. If you cannot locate the document, use the return address on the check envelope and ask the company to send you a copy of the plan. Also request that they forward to you any claim form that may be required in order for the survivor or beneficiary to receive benefits under that pension plan or policy.

If the pension/annuity check is direct deposited to the decedent's account, then ask the bank to assist you in locating the company and notifying the company of the death.

DECEDENT WITH AN IRA or a QUALIFIED RETIREMENT PLAN ("QRP")

Anyone who is a beneficiary of an Individual Retirement Account ("IRA") or QRP needs to keep in mind that in general no income taxes have been paid on monies placed in an IRA or QRP account. Once monies are withdrawn, significant taxes may be due. You need to learn what options are available to you as a beneficiary of the plan and the tax consequences of each option. You will need to ask an accountant how much will be due in taxes for each option. Once you know all the facts, you will be able to make the best choice for your circumstance.

 **SPOUSE** If the spouse is the beneficiary of the decedent's IRA account, then there are special options available. The spouse has the right to withdraw the money from the account or roll it over into the spouse's own retirement account. Although the employer can explain options that are available, the spouse still needs to understand the tax consequence of choosing any given option. It is important to consult with an accountant to determine the best way to go.

If the decedent had a QRP, the plan may permit the spouse to roll the balance of the account into a new IRA. The spouse needs to contact the decedent's employer for an explanation of the plan and all the options that are available at this time.

NOTIFYING IRS

THE FINAL INCOME TAX RETURN

The decedent's final income tax return (IRS form 1040) needs to be filed by April 15th of the year following the year in which he died. The state income tax is filed at the same time (MCL 206.315). The surviving spouse can file a final joint return. If there is no surviving spouse, then it is the Personal Representative's job to file all tax returns.

If no Probate procedure is necessary, then whoever inherits the decedent's property needs to file. If you have a joint account with the decedent, you may want to keep the account open until you determine whether the decedent is entitled to an income tax refund. See Chapter 6 for an explanation of how to obtain a refund.

THE GOOD NEWS

Monies inherited from the decedent are generally not counted as income to you, so you do not pay federal income tax on those monies. If the monies you inherit later earn interest or income for you, then of course you will report that income as you do any other type of income.

BENEFICIARY OF A
MICHIGAN HOMESTEAD

People who own a residence in Michigan are entitled to a homestead tax exemption, provided they occupy the homestead as their primary residence. If the homestead is transferred to a new owner through a sale or inheritance, then the new owner must obtain his own homestead tax exemption. If the new owner does not occupy the property as his Michigan homestead then the owner must notify the Michigan Department of Treasury of the transfer; and must, within 90 days, give up the homestead tax exemption by filing a Notice of Rescission.

It is important to file the Notice of Rescission within 90 days of the date of ownership, which in many cases is the date of the decedent's death (See Chapter 5 for an explanation of who owns the property when the decedent dies). Those who fail to notify the Michigan Department of Treasury within the 90 days may be fined up to $200 (MCL 211.7cc).

You can get the Notice of Rescission form by calling the Michigan Department of Treasury at (800) 487-7000 or you can download the form from the Internet:

 MICHIGAN DEPT. OF TREASURY WEB SITE
http://www.treasury.state.mi.us

SPOUSE ▸ SELLING THE HOME

In the tough "ole days" the IRS used to allow Capital Gains Tax exclusion (up to $125,000) on the sale of one's homestead (the principal residence). A person had to be 55 or older to take advantage of the exclusion, and it was a once-in-a-lifetime tax break. If a married couple sold their home and took the exclusion it was "used up" and no longer available to either partner.

In these, the good times, the IRS allows you to sell your homestead and up to $250,000 ($500,000 for a married couple) of the home-sale profit is tax free (IRC Section 121 B 3). There is no limit on the number of times you can use the exclusion, provided you own and live in the homestead at least 2 years prior to the sale.

If the decedent and his spouse used their "once in a lifetime" homestead tax exclusion, with this new law, the surviving spouse can sell the homestead and once again take advantage of a tax break.

AN ESTATE TAX FOR THE WEALTHY

The **Taxable Estate** of the decedent is the total value of all of his property, as of his date of death. This includes real property (homestead, vacant lots, etc.) and personal property (cars, life insurance policies, business interests, securities, IRA accounts, etc.). It includes property held in the decedent's name alone, as well as property that he held jointly or in trust for another.

An **Estate Tax** is a tax imposed by the federal and state government for the transfer of property at death. There is a federal **Gift Tax** on gifts given during a person's lifetime that exceed $10,000 per person, per year. Should a gift be given that exceeds $10,000, that gift must be reported to the IRS, but no tax need be paid unless the total value of gifts made in excess of $10,000 previously made by that person, exceeds a certain amount as set by the government. Once a person dies the cumulative value of gifts reported to IRS in excess of $10,000 per year is added to the decedent's Taxable Estate. No federal Estate Tax need be paid unless the combined sum exceed the Exemption Value as set by the federal government. This amount is scheduled to increase as follows:

YEAR	EXEMPTION VALUE
2002-2003	$1,000,000
2004-2005	$1,500,000
2006-2008	$2,000,000
2009	$3,500,000

There is an unlimited marital tax deduction for property transferred to the surviving spouse; so in most cases, no Estate Tax need be paid if the decedent was married. Regardless of whether taxes are due, federal and state Estate Tax returns must be filed whenever the decedent's estate exceeds the Exemption Value in effect as of his date of death (MCL 205.232).

The current federal Estate Tax is scheduled to be phased out in the year 2010, but a new Capital Gains Tax is scheduled for 2010 that may prove even more costly than the Estate Tax. The new Capital Gains Tax is related to the way inherited property is evaluated by the federal government. Real and personal property is inherited at a "step up" in basis. This means that if the decedent purchased an item that is worth more than when he purchased it, the beneficiary will inherit the property at its fair market value as of the decedent's date of death. For example, suppose the decedent bought stock for $20,000 and it is worth $50,000 as of the date of death, the beneficiary takes a step-up in basis of $30,000; i.e., he inherits the stock at the $50,000 value. If the beneficiary sells the stock for $50,000, he pays no Capital Gains tax. If the beneficiary holds onto the stock and later sells it for $60,000, the beneficiary will pay a Capital Gains tax only on the $10,000 increase in value since the decedent's death.

Up to 2009, there is no limit to the amount you can take as a step-up in basis. But in 2010 caps are set in place. The surviving spouse is allowed to take a step-up in basis of up to 4.3 million dollars. Property inherited by anyone else is allowed a 1.3 million dollar step-up in basis. Significant Capital Gains taxes could result. For example, suppose in 2010 you inherit a business from your father that he purchased for $100,000 and it is now worth 2 million dollars. There is a capital gain of 1.9 million dollars, but you are allowed a step-up in basis of only 1.3 million. $600,000 of your inheritance is subject to a Capital Gains tax.

No one knows how the new law will be applied in 2010, but it could well be that the Capital Gains tax on your inheritance turns out to be the same as, if not more than, what you would have paid in Estate Taxes, before they were "phased out."

THE UN-UNIFIED GIFT TAX

As explained on page 36, the Gift Tax is unified with the Estate Tax so that if you give a gift to someone in excess of $10,000, the amount over $10,000 is added to your Taxable Estate. Up until the change in the law, you did not need to pay a Gift Tax during your lifetime unless the amount given during your lifetime exceeded the Exemption Value. That changes in 2004. In 2004, the Exemption Value for the Estate Tax goes up to $1,500,000, but the Exemption Value for the Gift Tax remains at $1,000,000.

Specifically, if you make a gift to anyone of more than $10,000 per year, the amount over $10,000 must be reported to the IRS. The IRS keeps a running count of the reported values. As of 2004, once the sum of all of your reported values exceed $1,000,000, you will pay a Gift Tax on any amount that you give during your lifetime that exceeds $10,000 per person per year.

Special Situation ▷ DECEDENT WITH A TRUST

If the decedent was the Grantor (or Settlor) of a Trust, then he was probably managing the Trust as Trustee during his lifetime. The Trust document should name a *Successor Trustee* to manage the Trust now that the Grantor is deceased. The Trust document may instruct the Successor Trustee to make certain gifts once the Grantor dies or the Trust document may direct the Successor Trustee to hold money in Trust for a beneficiary of the Trust.

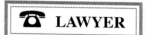

☎ LAWYER — IF YOU ARE SUCCESSOR TRUSTEE

If you are the Successor Trustee then in addition to following the terms of the Trust, you are required to obey all of the laws of the state of Michigan relating to the administration of the Trust. For example, Michigan law requires that, within 28 days of your acceptance of the Trust, you inform each beneficiary of the Trust, in writing, of your name and address; and of the beneficiary's right to know about the terms of the Trust that affect that beneficiary (MCL 700.7303). You should consult with an attorney experienced in Estate Planning to help you administer the Trust according to the law and without any liability to yourself.

IF YOU ARE A BENEFICIARY

If you are a beneficiary of the Trust, then you need to obtain a copy of the Trust provisions that apply to you and learn how the Trust will be administered now that the Grantor or Settlor is deceased. Most Trust documents are written in "legalese," so you may want to employ your own attorney to review the Trust, and explain your rights under that Trust.

NOTIFYING THE BUSINESS COMMUNITY

People and companies who were doing business with the decedent need to be notified of his death. This includes utility companies, credit card companies, banks, brokerage firms and any company that insured the decedent.

NOTIFY CREDIT CARD COMPANIES
You need to notify the decedent's credit card companies of the death. If you can find the contract with the credit card company check to see whether the decedent had credit card insurance. If the decedent had credit card insurance, then the balance of the account is now paid in full. If you cannot find the contract contact the company and get a copy of the contract along with a statement of the balance due as of the date of death.

DESTROY DECEDENT'S CREDIT CARDS
You need to destroy all of the decedent's credit cards. If you hold a credit card jointly with the decedent, then it is important to waste no time in closing that account and opening another in your name only.

That's something Barbara knows from hard experience. She and Hank never married but they did live together for several years before he died from liver disease. Hank came from a well to do family so he had enough money to support himself and Barbara during his long illness. Hank put Barbara on all of his credit card accounts so that she could purchase things when he became too ill to go shopping with her. After the funeral, Barbara had a gathering of friends and family at their apartment. Barbara was so preoccupied with her loss that she never noticed that Hank's credit cards were missing until the bill started coming in.

Barbara did not know who ran up the bills on Hank's credit cards during the month following his death. It was obvious that Hank's signature had been forged — but who forged it? One credit card company suspected that it might have been Barbara herself. Because the cards were held jointly, Barbara became liable to either pay the debts or prove that she did not make the purchases. She was able to clear her credit record but it took several months and she had to employ an attorney to do so.

NOTIFY INSURANCE COMPANIES

Examine the decedent's financial records to determine the name and telephone number of all of the companies that insured the decedent or his property. This includes real property insurance, motor vehicle insurance, health insurance and life insurance.

MOTOR VEHICLE INSURANCE
Locate the insurance policy for all motor vehicles owed by the decedent (car, truck, snowmobile, boat, airplane) and notify the insurance company of the death. Determine how long insurance coverage continues after the death. Ask the insurance agent to explain what things are covered under the policy. Is the motor vehicle covered for all types of casualty (theft, accident, vandalism, etc.) or is coverage limited in some way?

If you can continue coverage, then determine when the next insurance payment is due. Hopefully, the car will be sold or transferred to a beneficiary before that date, but if not, you need to arrange for sufficient insurance coverage during the Probate procedure.

ACCIDENTAL DEATH

If the decedent died as a result of an accident, then check for all possible sources of accident insurance coverage including his homeowner's policy. Some credit card companies provide accident insurance as part of their contract with their card holders.

If the decedent died in an automobile accident, check to see whether he was covered by any type of travel insurance, such as rental car insurance. If he belonged to an automobile club, such as AAA, then check whether he had accident insurance as part of his club membership.

LIFE INSURANCE COMPANIES

If the decedent had life insurance, then you need to locate the policy and notify the company of his death. Call each life insurance company and ask what they require in order to forward the insurance proceeds to the beneficiary. Most companies will ask you to send them the original policy and a certified copy of the death certificate.

Send the original policy by certified mail or any of the overnight services that require a signed receipt for the package. Make a copy of the original policy for your records before mailing the original policy to the company.

IF YOU CANNOT LOCATE THE POLICY

If you know that the decedent was insured, but you cannot locate the insurance policy, you can contact the company and request a copy of the policy. A tougher question is how to locate the policy if you can't find the policy and do not know the name of the insurance company. The American Council of Life Insurers offers suggestions that you may find helpful at the Missing Policy Inquiry page of their Web site:

AMERICAN COUNCIL OF LIFE INSURERS WEB SITE
http://www.acli.com

IF YOU CANNOT LOCATE THE COMPANY

If you cannot locate the insurance company it may be doing business under another name or it may no longer be doing business in the state of Michigan. Each state has a branch of government that regulates insurance companies doing business in that state. If you are having difficulty locating the insurance company call the Department of Insurance in the state where the policy was purchased and ask for assistance in locating the company. In Michigan you can call the Financial and Insurance Services at (517) 373-0240.

EAGLE PUBLISHING COMPANY OF BOCA has the telephone number for the Department of Insurance for each state at their Web site:

EAGLE PUBLISHING COMPANY OF BOCA WEB SITE
http://www.eaglepublishing.com

WORK RELATED INSURANCE

If the decedent was employed, then check his records for information about work related benefits. He may have survivor benefits from a company or group life insurance plan and/or a retirement plan. Also check with the employer about company benefits. If the decedent belonged to a union, then contact them to determine whether there are any union benefits.

The decedent may have belonged to a professional, fraternal or social organization such as the local Chamber of Commerce, a Veteran's organization, the Kiwanis, AARP, the Rotary Club, etc. If he belonged to any such organization check to see whether the organization provided any type of insurance coverage.

 **BUSINESS OWNED BY DECEDENT**

If the decedent owned his own company or was a partner in a company he may have purchased "key man" insurance. Key man insurance is a policy designed to protect the company should a valuable employee become disabled or die. Benefits are paid to the company to compensate the company for the loss of someone who is essential to the continuation of the business. Ultimately the policy benefits those who inherit the business.

If the decedent had an ownership interest in an ongoing business (sole proprietor, shareholder or partner) there may be a shareholder's or partnership agreement requiring the company to purchase the decedent's share of the business. The Personal Representative's attorney needs to investigate to see if there was a key man insurance policy and/or such purchase agreement.

CORPORATE OWNER OR RESIDENT AGENT

If the decedent was the sole owner and officer of a corporation then the Michigan Corporations Division needs to be notified of the change. There will need to be a Probate procedure to determine the new owner of the company so it may take some period of time before new officers and directors are identified.

The law requires each corporation to continuously maintain an Agent who resides in this state. If the decedent was the Resident Agent of a corporation, then a new Resident Agent needs to be appointed as soon as is practicable (MCL 450.1241, 450.1242).

Forms to change officers, directors and the Resident Agent can be obtained by calling the Corporation Division at (517) 241-6470 or by writing to:

Bureau of Commercial Services
Corporation Division
P.O. Box 30054
Lancing, MI   48909

Or from their Web site:

CORPORATION DIVISION WEB SITE
http://www.cis.state.mi.us/bcs/corp

If you were not actively involved in running the business, then you might request a status report of the company. The report will show whether the corporation is in good standing in the state of Michigan; i.e. whether their filing fees are current and the name and address of the Resident Agent of the company. You can get this information by calling the Corporation Division at the above number.

HOMEOWNER'S INSURANCE

If the decedent owned his own home, then check whether there is sufficient insurance coverage on the property. The decedent may have neglected to increase his insurance as the property appreciated in value. If you think the property may be vacant for some period of time, then it is important to have vandalism coverage included in the policy. Once the property is sold, or transferred to the proper beneficiary, you can have the policy discontinued or transferred to the new owner. The decedent's estate should receive a rebate for the unused portion of the premium.

MORTGAGE INSURANCE

If the decedent had a mortgage on any parcel of real estate that he owned, he might have arranged with his lender for an insurance policy that pays off the mortgage balance in the event of his death. Look at the closing statement to see if there was a charge for mortgage insurance. Also check with the lender to determine if such a policy was purchased.

If the decedent was the sole owner of the property, then the beneficiary of that property needs to make arrangements to continue payment of the mortgage until title to the property is transferred to that beneficiary.

NOTIFY THE HOMEOWNER'S ASSOCIATION

If the decedent owned a condominium or a residence regulated by a homeowner's association, then the association will need to be notified of the death. Once the property is transferred to the proper beneficiary, he/she will need to contact the association to learn of the rules and regulations regarding ownership and to arrange to have notices of dues and assessments forwarded to the new owner.

HEALTH INSURANCE

The Health Insurance carrier probably knows of the death, but it is a good idea to contact them to determine what coverage the decedent had under that insurance plan. If you cannot find the original policy, have the insurance company send you a copy of the policy so that you can determine whether medical treatment given to the decedent before his death was covered by that policy.

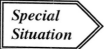

Special Situation **DECEDENT ON MEDICARE**

If the decedent was covered by Medicare, you do not need to notify anyone, but you do need to know what things were covered by Medicare so that you can determine what medical bills are (or are not) covered by Medicare. The publication **MEDICARE AND YOU** explains what things are covered. The book is available in regular print (Publication HCFA 10050) and in large print (Publication HCFA 10050-LE). You can get the book by writing to the

U.S. GOVERNMENT PRINTING OFFICE
U.S. Dept. of Health and Human Services
Health Care Financing Administration
7500 Security Boulevard
Baltimore, MD 21244-1850

You can also find the publication on the Internet:

MEDICARE WEB SITE
http:/www.medicare.gov

SPOUSE	THE SPOUSE'S HEALTH INSURANCE

If the spouse of the decedent is insured under Medicare, then the death does not affect the coverage of the surviving spouse. If the spouse is not covered by Medicare but has her own health insurance that also covered the decedent, then the spouse needs to notify the employer of the death because this may affect the cost of the plan to the employer and/or the spouse.

If the spouse was covered under the decedent's policy, then he/she needs to arrange for new coverage. There are federal laws that ensure continued coverage under the decedent's policy for a period of time. If the decedent was employed by a federally regulated company (usually a company with at least twenty employees) then under the Consolidated Omnibus Budget Reconciliation Act ("COBRA") the employer must make the company health plan available to the surviving spouse and any dependent child of the decedent for at least 36 months.

The employer is required to give notice to the surviving spouse that the spouse and/or dependent child have the right to continue coverage under the decedent's health plan. The spouse and/or child have 60 days from the date of death or 60 days after the employer sends notice (whichever is later) to tell the employer whether the surviving spouse and child wish to continue with the health insurance plan (29 USC 18 Sec. 1162, 1163).

SPOUSE'S HEALTH INSURANCE (continued)

The only problem with continued coverage may be the cost. Before the death, the employer may have been paying some percentage of the premium. The employer has no such duty after the death unless there was some employment agreement stating otherwise.

Under COBRA, the employer may charge the spouse for the full cost of the plan plus a 2% administrative fee. If you have a question about your coverage under COBRA, you can call the U.S. Department of Labor ("DOL") at (800) 998-7542 and ask for the number of your local DOL office. You can also ask that they send you their publication HEALTH BENEFITS UNDER COBRA; or you can visit their Web site for more information:

 DEPARTMENT OF LABOR WEB SITE
http://www.dol.gov/dol/pwba

Whether or not health insurance coverage falls under COBRA, it is important that the surviving spouse contact the employer, and the insurer, to learn of his/her options relating to continued coverage, or converting to a new health insurance policy, as soon as is practical after the death.

NOTIFY ADVERTISERS

Probably the last in the world to learn of the decedent's death is the direct mail advertiser. Advertisers are nothing if not tenacious. It is not uncommon for advertisements to be mailed to the decedent for more than ten years after the death. It is not because the advertiser is trying to sell something to the decedent, but rather the people who prepare (and sell) mailing lists do not know that the person is dead.

Those who sell mailing lists may not be motivated to update the list because of the cost of doing the necessary research; and maybe even because the price of the mailing list may be based on the number of people on the list. Even those who compose their own list may decide it is less costly to mail to everyone, than take the time (and money) to update the list.

If it gives you pleasure to think of advertisers spending substantial sums for nothing, then that is what you should do (nothing). But for those of you who wince each time you see another piece of mail addressed to the decedent, you can write to the Direct Marketing Association and ask that the name be deleted from all mailing lists: Mail Preference Service
Direct Marketing Association
P.O. Box 9008
Farmingdale, NY 11735

You will need to give them the decedent's complete address, including zip code and every name variation that the decedent may have used; for example:

Mr. Theodore James Jones	
Ted Jones	Ted J. Jones
T. J. Jones	T. James Jones, etc.

If the decedent was someone you named as beneficiary of your insurance policy, Will or Trust, brokerage account or pension plan, then you may need to name another beneficiary in his place:

INSURANCE POLICY ✍

If you named the decedent as the primary beneficiary of your life insurance policy, then check to see whether you named a contingent (alternate) beneficiary in the event that the decedent did not survive you. If not, then you need to contact the insurance company and name a new beneficiary. If you did name a contingent beneficiary, then that person is now your primary beneficiary and you need to consider whether you wish to name a new contingent beneficiary at this time.

HEALTH INSURANCE POLICY ✍

If the decedent was covered under your health insurance policy, then your employer and the health insurer need to be notified of the death because this may affect the cost of the plan to you and/or your employer.

WILL OR TRUST ✍

Most Wills provide for a contingent beneficiary in the event that the person named as beneficiary dies first. If you named the decedent as your beneficiary, then check to see whether you named an alternate beneficiary. If not, you need to have your attorney revise your Will and name a new beneficiary.

Similarly, if you are the Grantor or Settlor of a Trust and the decedent was one of the beneficiaries of your Trust, then check the Trust document to see if you named an alternate beneficiary. If not, contact your attorney to prepare an amendment to the Trust, naming a new beneficiary.

BANK AND SECURITIES ACCOUNTS ✍

If the decedent was a beneficiary of your bank or securities account, or if the decedent was a joint owner of your bank account or securities account, then it is important to contact the financial institution and tell them about the death. You may wish to arrange for a new beneficiary or joint owner at this time.

PENSION PLANS ✍

If the decedent was a beneficiary under your pension plan, then you need to notify them of his death and name a new beneficiary. Many pension plans require that you notify them within a set period of time (usually 30 days) so it is important to notify them as soon as you are able. If the decedent was a beneficiary of your Individual Retirement Account ("IRA") or of your Qualified Retirement Plan ("QRP") and you did not provide for an alternate beneficiary, then you need to name someone at this time.

Before you choose an alternate beneficiary, it is important that you understand all of the options available to you. Not an easy task. There are many complex government regulations relating to IRA and QRP accounts. And even if you believe you understood your options when you set up your account, they are scheduled to be changed beginning in 2002. You can read about the proposed regulations under 42 U.S.C 401(a)(9) in the *Federal Register* that was published on January 17, 2001, but unless you have an extensive tax background, it is just so much "legalese," i.e., incomprehensible without a professional to translate it into plain English.

Your choice of beneficiary can impact the amount of money you can withdraw each month, so it is important to consult with your accountant or tax attorney or financial planner, before you make your election.

NOTIFYING CREDITORS

If a Probate procedure is necessary and the decedent owed money, then it is the job of the person appointed as Personal Representative to notify the decedent's creditors of the death. The attorney who handles the Probate will explain to the Personal Representative how notice is to be given.

If no Probate procedure is necessary, then the next of kin can notify the creditors of the death, but before doing so, read Chapter 4: WHAT BILLS NEED TO BE PAID? That chapter explains what bills need to be paid and who is responsible to pay them.

Before any bill can be paid you need to know whether the decedent left any assets that could be used to pay those debts. The next chapter explains how to identify, and then locate all of the property owned by the decedent.

Locating the Assets

It is important to locate the financial records of the decedent and then carefully examine those records. Even the partner of a long-term marriage should conduct a thorough search because the surviving spouse may be unaware of all that was owned (or owed) by the decedent.

It is not unusual for a surviving spouse to be surprised when learning of the decedent's business transactions, especially in those cases where the decedent had control of family finances. One such example is that of Sam and Henrietta. They married just as soon as Sam was discharged from the army after World War II. During their marriage, Sam handled all of the finances giving Henrietta just enough money to run the household.

Every now and again Henrietta would think of getting a job. She longed to have her own source of income and some economic independence. Each time she brought up the subject Sam would loudly object. He had no patience for this new "woman's lib" thing. Sam said he got married to have a real wife — one who would cook his meals and keep house for him.

Henrietta was not the arguing type. She rationalized, saying that Sam had a delicate stomach and dust allergies. He needed her to prepare his special meals and keep an immaculate house for him. Besides, Sam had a good job with a major cruise line and he needed her to accompany him on his frequent business trips.

Once Sam retired, he was even more cautious in his spending habits. Henrietta seldom complained. She assumed the reason for his "thrift" was that they had little money and had to live on his pension.

They were married 52 years when Sam died at the age of 83. Henrietta was 81 at the time of his death. She was one very happy, very angry and very aged widow when she discovered that Sam left her with assets worth well over a million dollars!

LOCATING RECORDS

As you go through the papers of the decedent you may come across documents that indicate property ownership, such as bank registers, stock or bond certificates, insurance policies, brokerage account statements, etc. Place all evidence of ownership in a single place. You will need to contact the different companies in order to transfer title to the proper beneficiary. Chapter 5 explains how to identify the proper beneficiary of the decedent's property. Chapter 6 explains how to transfer the property to that beneficiary.

You may also need to produce evidence of the decedent's personal relationships, such as a marriage certificate, birth certificate, or naturalization papers, a Final Judgement of Divorce, military personnel records, etc. If you cannot locate his marriage certificate or birth certificate, you can get a certified copy of those records from the Vital Records office in the state where the event took place. See page 24 for Michigan's Vital Records. You can find the location and telephone number for other states by calling information or from the Internet by using your favorite search engine to locate Vital Records.

You can obtain a copy of a deceased Veteran's military record by writing to:

The National Personnel Records Center
Military Personnel Records
9700 Page Avenue
St. Louis, MO   63132-5100

They will send you form SF 180 to complete. You can get the form from the Internet at http://www.cem.va.gov
or from the National Archives and Records Administration Fax-On-Demand system. Dial (301) 713-6905 and request document number 2255.

COLLECT AND IDENTIFY KEYS

The decedent may have kept his records in a safe deposit box, so you may find that your first job is to locate the keys to the box. As you go through the personal effects of the decedent, collect and identify all the keys that you find. If you come across an unidentified key, it could be a key to a post office box (private or federal) or a safe deposit box located in a bank or in a private vault company. You will need to determine whether that key opens a box that contains property belonging to the decedent or whether the key is to a box no longer in use. Some ways to investigate are as follows:

☑ CHECK BUSINESS RECORDS

If the decedent kept receipts, look through those items to see if he paid for the rental of a post office or safe deposit box. Also, look at his check register to see if he wrote a check to the Postmaster or to any safe deposit or vault company. Look at his bank statements to see if there is any bank charge for a safe deposit box. Some banks bill separately for a safe deposit box so check with all of the banks in which the decedent had an account to determine whether he had a safe deposit box with that bank.

☑ CHECK THE KEY TYPE

If you cannot identify the key, then take it to each local locksmith and ask whether anyone can identify the type of facility that uses such keys. If that doesn't work, go to each bank, post office and private safe deposit boxes located in places where the decedent shopped, worked or frequented and ask whether they use the type of key that you found.

☑ CHECK THE MAIL

Check the mail over the next several months to see if the decedent receives a statement requesting payment for the next year's rental of a post office or safe deposit box.

FORWARD THE DECEDENT'S MAIL

You may find evidence of a brokerage account, bank account, or safe deposit box by examining correspondence addressed to the decedent. If the decedent was living alone, then have the mail forwarded to the person he named as Personal Representative of his Will. If the decedent did not leave a Will then the mail should be forwarded to his next of kin. Call the Postmaster and ask him/her to send you the necessary forms to make the change. Request that the mail be forwarded for the longest period allowed by law (currently one year).

The decedent may have been renting a post office box at his local post office branch or perhaps at the branch closest to where he did his banking. Ask the Postmaster to help you determine whether the decedent was renting a post office box. If so, then you need to locate the key to the box so that you can collect the decedent's mail.

Special Situation **LOST POST OFFICE BOX KEY**

If the decedent had a post office box and you cannot locate the key, then contact the local postmaster and ask him/her what documentation is needed for you to gain possession of the mail in that box. As before, you will ask the Postmaster to have all future mail addressed to that box, forwarded to the Personal Representative, or if there is no Will, then to the decedent's next of kin.

WHAT TO DO WITH CHECKS

You may receive checks in the mail made out to the decedent. Social security checks, pension checks and annuity checks issued after the date of death need to be returned to the sender. See pages 28 and 30 of this book. Other checks need to be deposited. If a Probate procedure is necessary, then the Personal Representative will open a Probate Estate account and the checks should be deposited to that account.

It no Probate procedure is necessary, then the checks can be deposited to any account held in the name of the decedent. The decedent is not here to endorse the check, but you can deposit to his account by writing his bank account number on the back of the check and printing beneath it "FOR DEPOSIT ONLY."

The bank will accept such an endorsement and deposit the check into the decedent's account. If the check is significant in value and/or the decedent had different accounts that are accessible to different people, then there needs to be cooperation and a sense of fair play. If not, the dollar gain may not nearly offset the emotional turmoil. Such was the case with Gail. Her father made her a joint owner of his checking account to assist in paying his bills. He had macular degeneration and it was increasingly difficult for him to see. The father also had a savings account that was in his name only.

Gail's brother, Ken, had a good paying job in Miami. Even though he lived at a distance, Ken, his wife and two children always spent the Christmas holidays with his father. Gail's good cooking added to the festivities. Each winter, their father enjoyed leaving the cold Michigan winter to spend a few warm weeks in south Florida.

One January, the father treated himself to a first class round trip ticket to Miami. The ticket cost several hundred dollars. Just before the departure date, the father had a heart attack and died. Gail called the airline to cancel the ticket. They refunded the money in a check made out to her father. She deposited the check to the joint account.

As part of the Probate procedure, the money in the father's savings account was divided equally between Ken and his sister. Ken wondered what happened to the money from the airline tickets.

Gail explained "He paid for the tickets from the joint account, so I deposited the money back to that account. "

"Aren't you going to give me half?"

"Dad meant for me to have whatever was in that joint account. If he wanted you to have half of the money, he would have made you joint owner as well."

Ken didn't see it that way: "That refund was part of Dad's Probate estate. It should have been deposited to his savings account to be divided equally between us. Are you going force me to argue this in court?"

Gail finally agreed to split the money with Ken, but the damage was done.

Gail complains that holidays are lonely since her father died.

LOCATING FINANCIAL RECORDS

To locate the decedent's assets you need to find evidence of what he owned and where those assets are located. His financial records should lead you to the location of his assets so your first job is to locate those records. The best place to start the search is in the decedent's home. Many people keep their financial records in a single place but it is important to check the entire house to be sure you did not miss something.

CHECK THE COMPUTER

Don't overlook that computer sitting silently in the corner. It may hold the decedent's check register and all of the decedent's financial records. The computer may be programmed to protect information. If you cannot access the decedent's records, you may need to employ a computer technician or computer consultant who will be able to print out all of the information on the hard drive of the computer. You can find such a technician or consultant by looking in the telephone book under
COMPUTER SUPPORT SERVICES   or
COMPUTER SYSTEM DESIGNS & CONSULTANTS.

LOCATE TITLE TO MOTOR VEHICLE

You should find the decedent's original certificate of title and his car registration among his important papers, or perhaps in the glove compartment of the car. In many states, if monies are owed on the car, the lender takes possession of the original certificate of title until the loan is paid. This is not the case in Michigan, so even if there is a car loan, you should be able to locate the original certificate of title. If you cannot find it, then the decedent's surviving spouse can get a copy of the certificate of title by going to the local Secretary of State branch office. If the decedent was single, then whoever is appointed as Personal Representative can go to the branch office in the county of the decedent's residence and get a duplicate title. You can check to see whether monies are owed on the car at that time. If you live out of state, you can call the Michigan Secretary of State for the name and address of a local office at (517) 322-1166. The address and phone number of each branch office is also available on the Internet:

 MICHIGAN SECRETARY OF STATE WEB SITE
http://www.sos.state.mi.us/

THE LEASED CAR

You may find that the car is leased and not owned by the decedent. If so, contact the lessor and get a copy of the lease agreement. Once you have the lease, check to see whether the decedent had life insurance as part of the agreement. If he did, then the lease may now be paid in full and the beneficiary should be able to use the car for the remainder of the leasing period, or take title to the car, whichever option is available under the lease agreement. The Personal Representative (or the beneficiary of the car if no Probate is necessary) can send the death certificate to the leasing company with a copy of the contract and a letter requesting that transfer be made.

COLLECT DEEDS

Collect the deeds to all property owned by the decedent. Many people keep deeds in a safe deposit box. If you cannot find the deed in the decedent's home, then you need to determine whether he had a safe deposit box. If you know that the decedent owned real property (lot, residence, condominium, cooperative, time share, etc.) but you cannot locate the deed, then contact the Register of Deeds in the county where the property is located. The county Register of Deeds can provide you with a copy of the last recorded deed.

You will need to identify the parcel of land by giving the legal description of the land or its permanent parcel identification number. You can find this information on the last tax bill sent to the decedent. If you cannot find the last property tax bill, then call the tax collector's office and they will give you the information.

You can use the same procedure if you cannot locate the deed to property owned by the decedent in another state, namely, check with the recording department in the county where the property is located to obtain a copy of the deed.

> **Special Situation**

DECEDENT'S RESIDENTIAL LEASE

If the decedent was renting his residence, then he may have a written lease agreement. It is important to locate the lease because the decedent's estate may be responsible for payments under the lease. If you cannot locate the lease, then ask the landlord for a copy. If the landlord reports that there was no written lease, then verify that the decedent was on a month to month basis and then work out a mutually agreeable time in which to vacate the premises.

If a written lease is in effect, then determine the end of the lease period, and whether there was a security deposit. Ask whether the landlord will agree to cancel the lease on the condition that the property is left in good condition. If the landlord says that the estate is responsible to pay the balance of the lease, then it is prudent to have an attorney review the lease to determine what rights and responsibilities remain now that the tenant is deceased.

☎ **LAWYER**

DECEDENT'S ONGOING BUSINESS

If the decedent was the sole owner of a business, or if he owned a partnership interest in a business, the Personal Representative needs to contact the company accountant to obtain the company's business records. If there is a company attorney, then the attorney may be able to assist in obtaining the records. If you are a beneficiary of the estate, consider consulting with your own attorney to determine what rights and responsibilities you may have in the business.

COLLECT TAX RECORDS

The decedent's final state and federal income tax returns need to be filed and you will need to locate all of his tax records for the past 3 years. If you cannot locate his prior tax records, then check his personal telephone book and/or his personal bank register to see if he employed someone to prepare his taxes. If you can locate his tax preparer, then he/she should have a copy of those records.

If you are unable to locate the decedent's federal tax returns, then they can be obtained from the IRS. The IRS will send copies of the decedent's tax filings to anyone who has a *fiduciary relationship* with the decedent. The IRS considers the following people to be a fiduciary:

➤ the person appointed as the Personal Representative of the decedent's estate

➤ the Successor Trustee of the decedent's Trust

➤ if the person died *intestate* (without a Will), then whoever is legally entitled to possession of the decedent's property (See page 110 for Michigan's Intestate Laws).

The fiduciary can receive copies of the decedent's tax filings by notifying IRS that he/she is acting in a fiduciary capacity, and then requesting the copies.

To notify the IRS of the fiduciary capacity file Form 56:
NOTICE CONCERNING FIDUCIARY RELATIONSHIP

To request the copies, file IRS Form 4506:
REQUEST FOR COPY OR TRANSCRIPT OF TAX FORM
Your accountant can file these forms for you or you can obtain the forms from the IRS by calling (800) 829-3676 or you can download them from the Internet:

 IRS FORMS WEB SITE
http://www.irs.gov/forms_pubs/forms.html

LOCATE STATE INCOME TAX RETURN

If you cannot locate the decedent's state income tax return you can get a copy from the Michigan Department of Treasury. They will give copies to the Personal Representative upon written request to

MICHIGAN DEPARTMENT OF TREASURY
TREASURY BUILDING
LANSING, MI 48922

Before writing, you may want to call the Department of Treasury at (800) 487-7000 and ask what information or document they require in order for you to obtain a copy of the decedent's state tax return.

LOCATE OUT OF STATE ACCOUNTS

If the decedent had out of state bank or brokerage accounts, then you might be able to locate them if they mail the decedent monthly or quarterly statements. Not all institutions do so, but all institutions are required to send out an IRS tax form 1099 each year giving the amount of interest earned on that account. Once the forms come in, you will learn the location of all of the decedent's active accounts.

FINDING LOST/ ABANDONED PROPERTY

If the decedent was forgetful, he may have money in a lost bank account or abandoned safe deposit box. Property that is unclaimed is turned over the to Michigan Department of Treasury after a period of time as set by Michigan law. The time period varies depending on the item:.

⏳   1 year for a utility deposit bank account

⏳   5 years for a bank account or safe deposit box

⏳   7 years for a travelers check or money order

Before doing so, the person or institution who is holding the property, must try to contact the owner at his/her last address. Once the Department receives the item, they will, within three years of receiving the property, sell the items and keep a record of the proceeds of the sale. If the owner (or their heir) later requests the property, then the state will give them the net proceeds of the sale (MCL 567.222, 567.226, 567.227, 567.229, 567.237, 567. 243).

You can determine whether there is a record identifying the decedent as the owner of abandoned property by calling (517) 335-4327 or writing to:

UNCLAIMED PROPERTY DIVISION
MICHIGAN DEPARTMENT OF TREASURY
LANSING, MI 48922

You can also get information from the Web site for the Michigan Department of Treasury:

   MICHIGAN DEPARTMENT OF TREASURY WEB SITE
http://www.treasury.state.mi.us/

CLAIMS FOR DECEDENT VICTIM OF HOLOCAUST

The New York State Banking Department has a special Claims Processing Office for Holocaust survivors or their heirs. The office processes claims for Swiss bank accounts that were dormant since the end of World War II. If the decedent was a victim of the Holocaust, you can get information about money that may be due to the decedent's estate by calling (800) 695-3318.

CLAIMS IN OTHER STATES

Each state has an agency or department that is responsible for handling lost, abandoned or unclaimed property located within that state. If the decedent had residences in other states, then call the UNCLAIMED or ABANDONED PROPERTY department to see if the decedent has unclaimed property in that state.

EAGLE PUBLISHING COMPANY OF BOCA lists telephone numbers for the unclaimed property division for each state at their Web site:

EAGLE PUBLISHING COMPANY OF BOCA
http://www.eaglepublishing.com

CLAIMS FOR IRS TAX REFUNDS

The IRS reports that some 90,000 tax refund checks representing 67.4 million dollars were returned to them as being not deliverable. They keep the information on file and will forward the full amount once they locate the taxpayer. You can determine whether they are holding a check for the decedent by calling the IRS at (800) 829-1040.

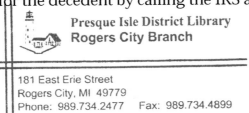

Presque Isle District Library
Rogers City Branch

181 East Erie Street
Rogers City, MI 49779
Phone: 989.734.2477   Fax: 989.734.4899

LOCATE CONTRACTS

If the decedent belonged to a health club or gym, he may have prepaid for the year. Look for the club contract. It will give the terms of the agreement. If you cannot locate the contract then contact the company for a copy of the agreement. If the contract was prepaid, then determine whether the agreement provides for a refund for the unused portion.

SERVICE CONTRACT
Many people purchase appliance service contracts to have their appliances serviced in the event that an appliance should need repair. If the decedent had a security system then he may have had a service contract with a company to monitor the system and contact the police in the event of a break-in.

If the decedent had a service contract, then you need to locate it and determine whether it can be assigned to the new owner of the property. If the contract is assignable, the new owner can reimburse the decedent's estate for the unused portion. If the contract cannot be assigned, then once the property is transferred, try to obtain a refund for the unused portion of the contract.

FILING THE WILL

Michigan law requires that whoever has possession of the decedent's original Will must, upon learning of the death, forward the Will promptly to the proper Probate Court. If the decedent was a resident of Michigan, then the Will should be forwarded to the Clerk in the county of his residence. If the decedent's primary residence was not in Michigan, then you need to check with an attorney to determine where the Will should be deposited (see page 74).

Michigan law requires that the Will be hand delivered to the Clerk of the Probate Court, or it can be sent to the Clerk by registered mail (MCL 700.2516).

If you have possession of the Will and can deliver it in person, then call the Clerk and ask for directions to the Probate Court. If you want to mail the Will, then ask the Clerk for the proper mailing address. Regardless of whether you mail it or hand carry the Will to the Clerk, it is important that you make a copy of the Will for your own records.

Once the Will is deposited with the court, the Clerk keeps it until someone begins a Probate procedure. It may be that no Probate procedure is necessary, in which case the Will remains in possession of the Probate court.

THE MISSING WILL

People tend to put off making a Will until they think they need to. For many, that need arises when they are elderly and/or seriously ill and have assets that they want to leave to someone. If the decedent was relatively young, with few assets, and you cannot find a Will, then he probably died without one. The probability of having a Will increases with age. A survey conducted for the American Association of Retired Persons ("AARP") found that 44% of those between the ages of 50 to 54 have a Will. This increases to 85% of those who are 80 and older. You can find more details of the survey at their Web site:

 AARP WEB SITE
http://research.aarp.org

Those who make a Will, usually tell the person that they appoint as Personal Representative of the existence of the Will. Chances are, that someone in the decedent's circle of family and friends, knows whether there is a Will. If you believe that the decedent had a Will, but you cannot find it, then there are at least three places to check out:

⇨ **THE DECEDENT'S ATTORNEY**
Look at the decedent's checkbook for the past few years and see whether he paid any attorney fees. If you are able to locate the decedent's attorney, then call and inquire whether the attorney ever drafted a Will for the decedent, and if so, whether the attorney has the original Will in his possession. If the attorney has the original Will, then ask the attorney to forward the Will to the Probate court. Asking the attorney to forward the Will to the court does not obligate you to employ the attorney should you later find that a Probate procedure is necessary.

⇨ **THE SAFE DEPOSIT BOX**

If you believe that the decedent had a Will but you cannot find it, then check to see whether the decedent had a safe deposit box. If he did, you will need to gain entry to that box to see whether the Will is in the box. See page 75 for an explanation of how to gain entry to the safe deposit box.

⇨ **THE PROBATE COURT**

Residents have the right to deposit their Will with the Probate Court in the county of their residence. At the time of deposit the Clerk will give the person a Certificate of Deposit. Once the Probate Court learns of the death, they will publicly open the Will and keep it until such time as someone begins the Probate procedure (MCL 700.2515).

Even if you cannot find a Certificate of Deposit, it is a good idea to check with the Clerk of the Probate Court in any county where the decedent resided. It could be that the Certificate is lost; or perhaps someone found the Will and deposited it with the Probate court.

 Special Situation — **WILL DRAFTED IN ANOTHER STATE OR COUNTRY**

The state of Michigan respects the laws of other states and countries. If the decedent was a resident of Michigan but his Will is drafted in another state or country and the Will is valid in that state or country, then it can be admitted to Probate the same as any Will drafted in the state of Michigan (MCL 700.2506).

If the Will is written in a foreign language, then it will need to be accompanied by a true and complete English translation before it can be admitted to Probate.

 **LAWYER**   A COPY BUT NO ORIGINAL

In Michigan, a person can revoke his Will simply by destroying or defacing the document (MCL 700.2507). If you have a copy of the Will and cannot find the original, the Court will presume that the decedent revoked that Will. You can ask the Judge to accept the copy into Probate, but you will need to prove to the Judge that the document is a true copy of the decedent's valid Will. You will also need to prove that the decedent had no intention of revoking that Will. These are not easy things to prove. You will need to employ an attorney experienced in Probate matters to present such proof to the Court.

 **LAWYER**   DECEDENT WITH
OUT OF STATE RESIDENCE

If the decedent had his residence in Michigan and owned property in another state, you may need to have a Probate procedure in Michigan and an ***ancillary*** (secondary) Probate procedure in the other state. It could be done the other way around; namely, you could have the Probate in the other state and the ancillary procedure in Michigan. If Probate is to be in another state, then the original Will needs to be delivered to the Probate court in that state. Before making the decision, the Personal Representative should consult with an attorney in each state to determine the best course of action. Convenience and cost are important considerations, but you also need to consider that each state has its own tax structure and Probate statutes. Ask each attorney whether the location of the Probate procedure will have any effect on who is to inherit the property or how much the estate will be taxed.

ACCESSING THE SAFE DEPOSIT BOX

If the decedent rented a safe deposit box jointly with another, and each had free access to the box, then the surviving joint owner can go to the box and remove any or all of the contents of the box (MCL 487.721, 700.2517). If the decedent rented a safe deposit box so that only he had access to the box, then a Personal Representative will need to be appointed in order to gain access to the box. If it is suspected that the decedent had his Will and/or deed to his burial space in the safe deposit box, then any interested person can ask the Probate court to issue an order allowing those items to be removed from the box and delivered to the Probate Register.

The order will say that the safe deposit box must be opened in the presence of an officer of the company that leased the box. All those in attendance when the box is opened must sign a statement saying whether the Will or deed to the burial space was in the safe deposit; and that no other item was removed from the box. If the deed and/or Will are in the box, the person named in the order must, within 7 days, deliver the items to the Probate court.

If you need to enter the safe deposit box to get the Will or deed before the Personal Representative is appointed, then you need to apply to the Probate court in the county where the safe deposit box is located. It will cost $10 to have the order issued. Once you have the order giving you the right to examine the contents of the box, you should call the bank and make an appointment to have an officer of the bank present. You may also want to ask whether there is a charge for opening the box in the presence of a company officer (MCL 205.209, 700.2517).

Other than the Will, and deed to the burial lot, nothing else may be removed from a safe deposit box that is leased only in the decedent's name, until the court appoints a Personal Representative. The Personal Representative can get access to the decedent's safe deposit box with the Letters issued by the Probate court.

If the decedent leased a box jointly with another and the surviving joint owner does not remove all of the contents of the box, then the Personal Representative can go to the box and remove its contents — but with restrictions. The box must be opened in the presence of an officer of the bank or leasing company. All who are in attendance are required to sign a written statement saying what was removed by the Personal Representative. The Personal Representative is required to give a copy of that statement to the surviving joint owner(s) within 7 days (MCL 700.2517).

Now that you have located all of the decedent's property you may think that the next step is to determine who inherits the property. But some of that property may be needed to pay monies owed by the decedent; so the next step is to determine what, if any, bills need to be paid. And that is the topic of the next chapter.

What Bills Need To Be Paid? 4

The Personal Representative has the duty to be sure that all valid *claims against the estate* (demand for payment) are paid. If the decedent had debts, but no money or property, then of course, there is no way to pay the claim. The only remaining question is whether anyone else is responsible to pay the decedent's debts. If the decedent was married, then the first person the creditor will look to, is the decedent's spouse. To understand the basis of this expectation, you need to know a bit of the history of our legal system.

Our laws are derived from the English Common Law. Under early English Common Law, a single woman had the right to own property in her own name and also the right to contract to buy or sell property; but when she married, her legal identity merged with her spouse. She could not hold property free from her husband's claim or control. She could no longer enter into a contract without her husband's permission.

Once married, a woman became financially dependent on her husband. He, in turn, became legally responsible to provide his wife with basic necessities — food, clothing, shelter and medical services. If anyone provided basic necessities to his wife, then, regardless of whether the husband agreed to be responsible for the debt, he became obliged to pay for them. This law was called the **DOCTRINE OF NECESSARIES.**

States in America departed from English Common Law by enacting a series of Married Women's Rights Acts giving a married woman the right to own property and to contract in her own name.

In the United States, a series of Married Women's Rights Acts were passed giving a married woman the right to own property, and the right to enter into a contract (MCL 557.21, 557.23).

Court cases followed that tested whether the Doctrine of Necessaries still applied. Judges had to decide:

If a wife can own property and contract to pay for her own necessaries, should her husband be responsible for her debts, in the event that she does not have enough money to pay for them?

And if it is determined that the husband is responsible for his wife's necessaries, should she be responsible for his?

Some states, notably New Jersey, answered "Yes" to both questions. But in Michigan, the Supreme Court decided ". . . neither a husband nor a wife is liable, absent express agreement, for necessaries supplied to each other." *North Ottawa Hosp. v. Kieft*, 457 Mich. 394 (1998); 578 N.W. 2d. 267.

In Michigan, if the decedent was married and owed money for necessaries (or any other item) then the creditor cannot demand payment from the spouse unless the spouse agreed to be responsible for that debt.

JOINT DEBTS

A *joint debt* is a debt that two or more people are responsible to pay. Usually the contract or promissory note reads that both parties agree to *joint and several* liability, meaning they both agree to pay the debt and each of them, individually, agree to be pay the debt. A joint debt can also be in the form of monies owed by one person with payment guaranteed by another person. If the person who owes the money does not pay, then the *guarantor* (the person who guaranteed payment) is responsible to make payment.

Before paying a bill, determine whether it is the decedent's debt or a joint debt. Hospital bills, nursing home bills, funeral expenses, legal fees incurred because of the decedent's death are all debts of the decedent's estate. They are not joint debts unless someone guaranteed payment for the monies owed.

PAYING FOR THE JOINT DEBT

If another person is jointly responsible for monies owed by the decedent, then that bill should be paid from any joint account held with the decedent. If the joint debtor did not have a joint account with the decedent, then the joint debtor must pay the bill from his/her own funds.

SPOUSE	DEBTS THE SPOUSE MUST PAY

Loans signed by the decedent and his spouse are joint debts, as are charges on credit cards that both were authorized to use. Property taxes are a joint debt if the decedent and the spouse both owned the property.

JOINT PROPERTY BUT NO JOINT DEBT

Suppose all of the decedent's funds are held jointly with his spouse or a family member and the joint owner of the account did not agree to pay those debts. Can the creditor require that half of the joint funds be set aside to pay the debt? Or suppose all the decedent owned was some real property that he held jointly with someone — could the creditor force the sale of the property and require the decedent's "half" be used to pay the debt?

The answer to whether the decedent's creditor can require the joint owner of the property to use the decedent's share to pay the debt depends on how the joint property is titled. Michigan courts have ruled that if the property is held jointly *with right of survivorship*, then the surviving owner owns the property as of the date of death (*Albro v. Allen*, 434 Mich. 271 (1990), 454 N.W.2d 85).

If there is no right of survivorship, then the creditor has the right to demand that the decedent's share be used to pay his debt.

Under Michigan law, a bank or credit union account in two or more names is presumed to have rights of survivorship. Once a joint owner dies, the amount on deposit belongs to the surviving owner(s) (MCL 487.703, 490.56). There is an exception to that rule and that is the *Statutory Joint Account*. A Statutory Joint Account can be set up so that the surviving joint owner inherits the money in the account, however, as explained on the next page, monies in such an account can be used to pay the decedent's debts.

THE STATUTORY JOINT ACCOUNT

When a person opens a bank account, the bank will asks the person to sign a contract that sets out rights and responsibilities of the bank and of the owner of the account. Michigan has a standard Statutory Joint Account Contract. The form identifies:

- who can withdraw monies from the account
- who owns the monies in the account during the lifetime of the depositors
- who owns the monies in the account should one of the depositors die

Although the Statutory Joint Account is called a "joint account," it does not necessarily have any rights of survivorship. The Statutory Joint Account could set it up as a convenience account giving someone authority to write checks, but without any right of survivorship — or it could be set up so that each owner has a right of survivorship.

Under Michigan law, an owner's share of a Statutory Joint Account is available to pay the owner's debts both before and after death. If the decedent had a Statutory Joint Account and there is not enough money in his estate to pay for his debts, his creditors can require the surviving joint owner use as much of the account as was owned by the decedent to pay those bills. The funds can also be used compensate the surviving spouse for the share of the decedent's estate that the spouse is entitled to receive under Michigan law. Specifically, if decedent was married and there are not enough Probate funds to pay the statutory amount to the surviving spouse,*** the Personal Representative can require the decedent's share of the Statutory Joint Account be used to compensate the spouse (MCL 487.715, 487.718, 487.719).

*** See the example given on Page 124.

NO MONEY — NO PROPERTY

If the decedent owed money, then the debt needs to be paid from assets owned by the decedent — which leads to the next question "Did the decedent have anything in his own name when he died?"

If the decedent died without any money or property in his name, then there is no money to pay any creditor. The only question that remains is whether anyone else is liable to pay those bills. The issue of payment most often arises in relation to services provided by nursing homes. When a person enters a nursing home, he is usually too ill to speak for himself or even sign his name. In such cases, the nursing home administrator will ask the spouse or a family member to sign a battery of papers on behalf of the patient before allowing the patient to enter the facility. Buried in that battery of papers may be a statement that the family member agrees to be responsible for payment to the nursing home. If the family member refuses to guarantee payment and the patient's finances are limited, then the facility may refuse to admit the patient.

If a nursing home accepts Medicare or Medicaid payments, then, under the Federal Nursing Home Reform Law, the nursing home is prohibited from requiring a family member to guarantee payment as a condition of allowing the patient to enter that facility (USC Title 42 §1395I-3(c)(5)(A)(ii)). Nonetheless, it is common practice for a nursing home, in effect, to say "Either someone agrees to pay for the patient's bill or you need to find a different facility."

Their position is understandable in the light of the 1998 Michigan Supreme Court ruling that spouses are not responsible for their partner's debts (see page 78). Most nursing homes are business establishments and not charitable organizations. The nursing home must be paid for the services they provide or they soon will be out of business. For an insolvent patient, the solution to the problem is to have the patient admitted to a facility as a Medicaid patient.

But what if the decedent had some money when he entered the nursing home and you agreed to guarantee payment to the nursing home?

What if you feel that you were coerced into signing as a guarantor?

Are you now liable to pay the decedent's final nursing home bill if your family member died without funds?

An experienced Elder Law attorney will be able to answer these questions after examining the documents that you signed and the conditions under which the patient entered the nursing home.

PAYING THE DECEDENT'S BILLS

If the decedent's estate is solvent, i.e., there is money available to pay his debts, then it is the job of the Personal Representative to do so. Once the Probate procedure begins, all of the decedent's creditors will be given an opportunity to come forward and produce evidence showing how much is owed.

The Personal Representative needs to look at each unpaid invoice and decide whether it is a valid bill. The problem with making that decision is that the decedent is not here to say whether the decedent actually received the goods and services now being billed to his estate.

That is especially the case for medical or nursing care bills. An example of improper billing brought to the attention of this author was that of a bill submitted for a physical examination of the decedent. The bill listed the date of the examination as July 10th, but the decedent died on July 9th. Other incorrect billings may not be as obvious, so each invoice needs to be carefully examined.

If the Personal Representative decides to challenge a bill, and is unable to settle the matter with the creditor, then the Probate Court will decide whether the debt is valid and should be paid.

MEDICAL BILLS COVERED BY INSURANCE

If the decedent had health insurance you may receive an invoice stamped "THIS IS NOT A BILL." This means the health care provider has submitted the bill to the decedent's health insurance company and expects to be paid by them. Even though payment is not requested, it is important to verify that the bill is valid for two reasons:

➢ **LATER LIABILITY**

If the insurer refuses to pay the claim, the facility will seek payment from whoever is in possession of the decedent's property, and that may reduce the amount inherited by the beneficiaries.

➢ **INCREASED HEALTH CARE COSTS**

Regardless of whether the decedent was covered by a private health care insurer or Medicare, improper billing increases the cost of health insurance to all of us. Consumers pay high premiums for health coverage. We, as taxpayers, all share the cost of Medicare. If unnecessary or fraudulent billing is not checked, then ultimately, we all pay.

Special Situation   MEDICARE FRAUD

If you believe that you have come across a case of Medicare fraud, you can call the ANTI-FRAUD HOTLINE (800)447-8477 and report the incident to the Office of the Inspector General of the United States Department of Health and Human Services.

HOW TO CHECK MEDICARE BILLING

If the decedent was covered by Medicare, then an important billing question is whether the health care provider agreed to accept Medicare *assignment of benefits*, meaning that they agreed to accept payment directly from Medicare. If so, the maximum liability for the patient is **20%** of the amount determined as reasonable by Medicare. For example, suppose a doctor bills Medicare $1,000 for medical treatment of the decedent. If Medicare determines that a reasonable fee is $800, then the patient is liable for 20% of the $800 ($160).

Health care providers who do not accept Medicare assignment bill the patient directly. They can charge up to 15% more than the amount allowed by Medicare. If the decedent knew and agreed to be liable for the payment, then his estate may be liable for whatever Medicare doesn't pay. For example, if a doctor's bill is $1,000 and Medicare allows $800, then Medicare will reimburse the decedent's estate 80% of $800 ($640). The doctor may charge the estate 15% more than the $800 ($920) and the estate may be liable for the difference: $920 - $640 or $280.

To summarize:
For health care providers accepting Medicare assignment, the most they can bill the decedent's estate is 20% of what Medicare allows (not 20% of what they bill.)

Those who do not accept Medicare assignment, can bill 15% more than the amount allowed by Medicare. The decedent's estate may be liable for the difference between the amount billed and the amount paid by Medicare.

In either case, if the decedent had secondary health care insurance, then the secondary insurer may be responsible to pay for the difference.

DENIAL OF
MEDICARE COVERAGE

If the health care provider reports to you that services provided to the decedent are not covered by Medicare, or if the facility submits the bill to Medicare and Medicare refuses to pay, then check to see if you agree with that ruling by determining what services are covered under Medicare. See page 47 to get a publication on what is (or is not) covered.

If you have a specific question on coverage, you can call the State Health Insurance Assistance Program ("SHIP") in Michigan (800) 803-7174. Or you can call the national Medicare Hotline (800) 633-4227. English and Spanish speaking operators are available Monday through Friday from 8 a.m. to 4:30 p.m. For the hearing impaired call TTY/TDD call (877) 486-2048.

APPEALING THE DENIAL OF COVERAGE

If you believe that the decedent was wrongly denied coverage, then you can appeal that decision. You can call the Michigan Bar at (800) 968-0738 for a referral to an attorney experienced in Medicare appeals. Some attorneys work *pro bono* (literally for the public good; i.e. without charge) but most charge to assist in an appeal. Federal statute 42 U.S.C. §406(a)(2)(A) limits the amount an attorney may charge for a successful Medicare appeal to 25% of the amount recovered or

SOME THINGS ARE CREDITOR PROOF

Sometimes it happens that the decedent had money or property, but he also had a significant amount of debt. In such cases the beneficiaries may wonder whether they should go through a Probate procedure if there will be little, if anything, left after the creditors are paid. Before making the decision consider that some assets are protected under Michigan law:

✧ FEDERAL PENSION PLAN ✧

Monies in the decedent's Federal retirement plan are protected from the decedent's creditor. Such plans are identified by the Internal Revenue Code of 1986 as 401, 403(b), 408 or 408A. This includes the decedent's individual retirement accounts ("IRA") and individual retirement annuities. There are a few exceptions to the rule. The funds are not protected from a judgment associated with a divorce, separation or child support; so if the decedent owed back child support or alimony, then these pension funds are available to pay the debts (MCL 600.6023 (k)).

NO EXEMPTION FOR TAXES

In general, income taxes are not paid when money is placed in a retirement plan. Taxes are paid when the monies are withdrawn from the account regardless of whether the monies are withdrawn by the retiree or the person he named as beneficiary of the retirement plan. If you inherit money from the decedent's pension, annuity or retirement fund, then you need to consult with an accountant or an attorney to determine how much money needs to be set aside to pay taxes.

✧ THE HOMESTEAD ✧

Property owned and occupied in Michigan by a person as his/her main residence is called *homestead* property. The decedent's creditors will not be able to force the sale of the family homestead to pay the decedent's debts while any of his children are under the age of 18. If a decedent with a spouse and no children, leaves all or part of the homestead to his spouse, then the decedent's creditors cannot force the sale of the property unless the spouse remarries. The surviving spouse does not need to physically occupy the property. It can be rented out and the proceeds will go to the surviving spouse free of the decedent's debts. This homestead exemption is not available to a surviving spouse who is already the owner of a homestead.

Also, these exemptions do not apply to a mortgage on the property. Any mortgage on the homestead must continue to be paid; else the lender has the right to foreclose (MCL 600.6023).

✧ PROCEEDS FROM WRONGFUL DEATH SUIT ✧

If anyone committed a wrongful act against the decedent that caused injury to the decedent or led to his death, then regardless of whether that person is convicted of a crime, the Personal Representative may sue that person for a wrongful death. If successful, monies recovered will be used to reimburse the decedent's estate for medical bills and funeral expenses. Michigan law limits those who can be compensated for the loss to the spouse and next of kin as defined by Michigan's laws of Intestate Succession, or the stepchildren of the decedent, or to the beneficiaries of the decedent's Will or Trust. Whoever is compensated for the loss will take the money free from the decedent's creditors (MCL 600.2922, 700.3924).

✧ LIFE INSURANCE PAYABLE TO SPOUSE OR CHILD ✧

Proceeds of a life insurance policy or an annuity policy payable to the spouse or child (minor or adult) of the insured decedent is not available to pay monies owed by the decedent. The spouse and/or child receive these funds free of any claim of the decedent's creditors.

There is no limit on the amount of insurance proceeds, provided that the decedent did not purchased the policy with the intent of defrauding his creditors. For example, suppose the decedent owed more money than he could pay. If he used what funds he did have to purchase a life insurance policy, then his creditors could make a claim on whatever monies he used to buy the policy, plus interest on that money (MCL 500.2207).

✧ THERE IS A PRIORITY OF PAYMENT ✧

Not all Probate debts are equal. Michigan statute (MCL 700.3805) establishes an order of priority for payment of claims made against the decedent's estate:

1. COST OF ADMINISTRATION

Top priority goes to the cost of the Probate procedure including attorney's fees and fees charged by the Personal Representative.

2. FUNERAL EXPENSES

Second in priority are reasonable funeral and burial expenses.

3. HOMESTEAD ALLOWANCE

The decedent's spouse is entitled to a *Homestead Allowance* of $15,000. If there is no surviving spouse, then the decedent's minor and/or dependent children are entitled to the $15,000; which is divided equally between them. For those dying after December 31, 2000, a Cost Of Living Adjustment ("COLA") can be added to this amount. The Michigan Department of Treasury will publish the COLA each year. (MCL 700.1210, 700.2402)

4. FAMILY ALLOWANCE

The spouse and dependent children of the decedent are entitled to receive money for their maintenance while Probate is being conducted. This maintenance is called a *Family Allowance*. The Personal Representative can determine the amount of the allowance to be paid to a maximum of $18,000, plus the COLA as determined by the Michigan Department of Treasury. The Family Allowance can be paid in a single lump sum or in periodic installments. If the estate is not large enough to pay all of the valid claims, then the Family Allowance cannot last more than a year (MCL 700.2403, 700.2405).

5. EXEMPT PROPERTY

The decedent's spouse is entitled to household furniture, furnishings, appliances and automobile up to a net value of $10,000 plus the same cost of living adjustment as applied to the Homestead Allowance. If the decedent was single, then surviving children can share these items. If the decedent's exempt property does not equal $10,000, then the spouse, or child(ren), are entitled to any other asset of the estate to make up that $10,000 value. (MCL 700.1210, 700.2404).

6. FEDERAL TAXES

If monies or taxes are owed by the decedent to the federal government, and the monies owed have preference under federal law, then these debts are sixth in priority.

7. MEDICAL

Seventh in line for payment are the reasonable and necessary medical and hospital expenses of the decedent's last illness. This also includes compensation for those persons who were caring for the decedent during his illness.

8. STATE TAXES

Any debt or tax with priority under the laws of the state of Michigan are 8th in priority of payment.

9. ALL OTHER CLAIMS

Michigan law requires that claims against the Probate Estate be paid in the above order. There is no priority within each class. For example, suppose there was enough money to pay the first 6 classes of claims with $10,000 left over. If the decedent owed more than $10,000 in medical bills, then the $10,000 would be prorated among the claimants.

✧ THERE IS A STATUTE OF LIMITATIONS ✧

Finally, consider that there is a statute of limitations for bringing a claim against the Probate Estate of the decedent. The first job of the Personal Representative is to publish notice in a newspaper saying that the decedent died, that a Probate procedure is in progress, and that creditors have 4 months to file a claim. If the identity of a creditor is known, then the Personal Representative must give that creditor notice by mail. If a creditor fails to file a claim within four months after the date of the first publication, then his claim is barred (MCL 700.3801, 700.3803).

But what if no one starts a Probate procedure?
Michigan law states that if a claim is not filed within three years after the death, then that claim cannot be enforced against the estate, the Personal Representative, or any of the beneficiaries.

There are exceptions to the three-year limit such as mortgages and federal claims and certain liens on the decedent's property. But, in general, if no one begins a Probate procedure until three years have passed, then the beneficiaries may be able to obtain possession of the decedent's assets free from creditor claims.

Read on before you decide to wait out the three years.

 **LAWYER** ## DECEDENT WITH MUCH DEBT

If the decedent died leaving much debt and no property, then the solution is simple. No Probate, no one gets paid. But if the decedent had property and died owing a significant amount of money, his heirs may be tempted to wait the three year period and begin Probate at that time. Such a strategy may turn out to be more hassle than its worth. Some creditors are tenacious and will use whatever legal strategy is available in order to be paid. For example, if no one starts a Probate procedure within 42 days of the decedent's death, then a creditor can petition the court to have someone appointed as Personal Representative (MCL 700.3203).

Family members may object to having a creditor decide who gets to be Personal Representative, so there could be a court battle over who has priority to be appointed as Personal Representative. Once Probate begins there may be additional litigation regarding which bills should be paid and in what priority.

Court battles are expensive, emotionally as well as financially. Before you decide to wait out a creditor by postponing Probate, consult with an attorney experienced in Probate matters for his/her opinion about the best way to administer the estate.

MONIES OWED TO THE DECEDENT

Suppose you owed money to the decedent. Do you need to pay that debt now that he is dead? That depends on whether there is some written document that says the debt is forgiven once the decedent dies. For example, suppose the decedent lent you money to buy your home. If he left a Will saying that once he dies, your debt is forgiven, then you do not need to make any more payments. If you signed a promissory note and mortgage at the time you borrowed the money from the decedent, then the Personal Representative should sign the original promissory note "PAID IN FULL" and return the note to you. If the mortgage was recorded, then the Personal Representative should sign and record a satisfaction of mortgage.

If you owed the decedent money and there is no Will, or if there is a Will and no mention of forgiving the debt, then you still owe the money. If you borrowed the money from the decedent and his spouse, then you need to pay the debt to the spouse (MCL 557.151).

If you borrowed the money from the decedent only, then the debt becomes an asset to the estate of the decedent, meaning that you now owe the money to the decedent's estate. If you are one of the beneficiaries of the estate, you can deduct the money from your inheritance. For example, suppose your father left $70,000 in a bank account to be divided equally between you and your brother. If you owed your father $20,000, then your father's estate is really worth $90,000. Instead of paying the $20,000, you can agree to receive $25,000 from the bank account and have the $20,000 debt forgiven. Your brother will receive the remaining $45,000 in cash.

Who Are The Beneficiaries? 5

A question that comes up early on is who is entitled to the property of the decedent. To answer the question you first need to know how the property was titled (owned) as of the date of death.

There are three ways to own property. The decedent could have owned property jointly with another person; or in trust for another person; or the decedent could have owned property that was titled in his name only.

In general, upon the decedent's death:

Joint Property belongs to the surviving joint owner.

Trust Property belongs to the beneficiary
of the Trust.

Property owned by the **decedent only** is inherited
by the beneficiaries named in the Will.
If there is no Will, then the property goes to his heirs
according to Michigan's Laws of Intestate Succession.

NOTE ⇨ If the decedent was married, then his
spouse may have rights in his property.

This chapter explains each of these types of ownership in detail.

PROPERTY HELD JOINTLY

Bank accounts, securities, motor vehicles, real property can all be owned jointly by two or more people. If one of the joint owners dies, then the survivor(s) continue to own their share of the property. Who owns the share belonging to the decedent depends on how the joint ownership was set up:

THE JOINT BANK ACCOUNT

If a bank account is opened in two or more names, then each depositor is given a statement of the terms and conditions of the account. The statement will say whether each depositor has authority to make a withdrawal, or whether two signatures are necessary. Unless the account states differently, in Michigan, a joint account is a survivorship account (see page 80).

Each owner of a joint account owns as much of the account as was contributed by that person to the account. It is presumed that a married couple each own half of their joint account, regardless of who deposited the funds. If a survivorship account is held in three names and one owner dies, then the share owned by the decedent is divided equally between the surviving owners. Of course, either of the survivors can go to the bank and withdraw all of the funds in the account. With such an arrangement, the surviving owners need to cooperate with each other to divide the funds in the account equitably (MCL 490.56, 491.616).

JOINTLY HELD SECURITIES

You can determine whether the decedent owns a security alone or jointly with another by examining the face of the stock or bond certificate. If two names are printed on the certificate followed by a statement that the owners are "joint tenants with rights of survivorship ("JTWRS")," or if married as husband and wife, or as "tenant by the entireties," then the surviving owner can either cash in the security or ask the company to issue a new certificate in the name of the surviving owner (MCL 557.151).

A security held jointly without rights of survivorship, is held as a *Tenancy In Common.* Should one co-owner die, his share goes to whomever he named as beneficiary of his Will, or if no Will, then it goes to his heirs as determined by the Michigan Laws of Intestate Succession (see page 111).

Each state has its own securities regulations. If a security held in two or more names, was registered or purchased in another state, then you will need to contact the company to determine how the account was set up; i.e. with or without rights of survivorship.

If the decedent held his securities in a brokerage account, then the name of the owner of that account is printed on the monthly or quarterly brokerage statement. Not all brokerage firms print the name of a joint owner on the brokerage statement, so you need to contact the firm to determine whether there is a surviving joint owner, or perhaps a beneficiary of the account. Request a copy of the contract that is the basis of the account. The contract will show when the account was opened and the terms of the brokerage account.

JOINTLY HELD MOTOR VEHICLES

If a motor vehicle is held jointly, the name of each owner is printed on the title to the motor vehicle. If the title says **with full rights of survivor**, then should one person die, the survivor owns the car, 100%. If you are such surviving joint owner then you need to go to the Secretary of State Branch Office to change title and registration. You may wish to first call your local Branch Office to determine what documents you will need to take with you. If you are calling from out of state you can reach the Michigan Secretary of State at (517) 322-1166.

It is important to change title as soon as you are able. You might be able to get a reduced insurance rate if there is only one person insured under the policy. Also, should the surviving owner be involved in an accident, and title has officially been changed, then there is no question that the estate of the decedent is in no way liable for the accident.

If title to the car was held jointly but there are no rights of survivorship, then the decedent's "half" of the car goes to his estate in the same manner as a motor vehicle held in the decedent's name only.

MOTOR VEHICLE IN DECEDENT'S NAME ONLY

If the decedent's car was in his name only and he left a Will, then the car goes to the beneficiaries named in the Will. If the decedent died without a Will then the car goes to the next of kin as defined in the Michigan Laws of Intestate Succession. See page 111 for an explanation of the law. See Chapter 6 for an explanation of how to transfer title to the motor vehicle.

MICHIGAN REAL PROPERTY HELD JOINTLY

The name of the owner of real property is printed on the face of the deed. To determine whether the decedent owned the property jointly with another person, you need to look at the last recorded deed. (See page 64 if you cannot locate the deed.)

ROBERT TRAYNOR, a single man
whose address is 22 Lake Street, Hart, MI
conveys and warrants to
ROBERT TRAYNOR, JR. a married man and
HENRY TRAYNOR, a single man
as joint tenants
the real property with legal description

. . .

Robert Traynor is the ***Grantor*** of the deed. That means he transferred the property to Robert Jr. and Henry Traynor who are the ***Grantees*** and present owners of the property. Should one of the joint tenants die, then the surviving joint tenant owns the property 100%. Nothing need be done to establish the ownership, however the decedent's name remains on the deed.

Should the surviving owner want to transfer the property all he/she need do is record a certified copy of the death certificate to prove that he/she is now the sole owner (MCL 65.48). See page 141 for information about how to have the death certificate recorded.

🗎 DEED HELD AS TENANTS IN COMMON

If the Grantee of a deed identifies the decedent and another as **TENANTS IN COMMON** then the decedent's share belongs to whomever the decedent named as his beneficiary in his Will. If the decedent died without a Will, then the Michigan Laws of Intestate Succession determine who inherits the decedent's share of the property. See page 108 for an explanation of the law.

If the deed names two or more people as the Grantee and does not say whether they are "Joint Tenants" or "Tenants In Common" then according to Michigan Statute 554.44, they hold title as Tenants in Common. If property is owned by the decedent as a Tenant In Common, then a Probate procedure is necessary. The Personal Representative named in the Will or if no Will, then the next of kin, will need to employ an attorney experienced in Probate matters to record a new deed that identifies the rightful owners.

 **LAWYER** | THE AMBIGUOUS DEED

Most deeds clearly state whether there are rights of survivorship. But some deeds can be read two ways. For example, if Ruth White transferred property to her son and daughter and the deed read:
"Ruth White jointly with Ralph White and Susan Peters"

It could be that Ruth wanted Ralph and Susan to be Tenants in Common, so if one of them dies, their share goes their estate. It could be that Ruth intended that they all be joint tenants, but in Michigan, the word "jointly," by itself, is not sufficient to create a joint tenancy. Best to consult with an attorney if you have any question about how to interpret the deed.

▤ DEED WITH A LIFE ESTATE

A *life estate* interest in real property means that the person who owns the life estate has the right to live in that property until he/she dies. You can identify a life estate interest by examining the face of the deed. If somewhere on the face of the deed you see the phrase RESERVING A LIFE ESTATE to the decedent, then the Grantee(s) now own the property. For example, suppose the granting paragraph of the deed reads:

> PETER REILLY, a single man,
> whose address is
> 123 Main Street, Flint, Michigan
> conveys and warrants to
> to ROSE SMITH, a married woman,
>
> . . .
>
> RESERVING A LIFE ESTATE TO THE GRANTOR

Peter Reilly is the owner of the life estate. While he is alive, the Grantee (Rose Smith) has no right to occupy the property. Once Peter dies, Rose owns the property, and is free to take possession of the property or transfer it, as she sees fit.

As with a survivorship tenancy, nothing need be done to establish Rose's ownership of the property, however the death certificate should be recorded to show anyone who is examining title to the property that Rose now owns the property (see Page 141).

🗐 DEED HELD AS HUSBAND AND WIFE

If the Grantee on the deed is identified as a married couple, such as:

TODD AMES AND SUSAN AMES, HUSBAND AND WIFE or

TODD AMES AND SUSAN AMES, TENANTS BY ENTIRETY

then when one spouse dies, and providing they are married at the time of death, the surviving spouse owns the property 100%. As with a survivorship tenancy, a death certificate will need to be recorded so that anyone who is examining title to the property will know that the surviving spouse is now the sole owner of the property.

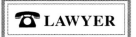 **DIVORCED PRIOR TO DEATH**

Once a couple divorce, all real property held by the couple as joint tenants or as Tenants by the Entirety becomes a Tenancy In Common (MCL 552.102).

If the decedent was divorced before he died, and the deed to property owned with his former spouse has not been changed, then unless the Final Judgment states otherwise, the former spouse has no right of survivorship in that property (MCL 700.2807). The decedent's half of the property descends to his heirs or beneficiaries and not to his former spouse. You will need to consult with an attorney to have a new deed prepared that identifies the new owners of the property.

SPOUSE ➤ AN INVISIBLE LIFE ESTATE

If the decedent was married and he held real property in his name only, then unless his widow gave up her *Dower* rights she has the right to a life estate in 1/3rd of all of the land that her husband owned during the time they were married. This means that regardless of what the deed says and regardless of who inherits the property, the spouse has the right to possess or to receive the profits from 1/3 or all of the decedent's real property, for so long as she lives. And this is so regardless of whether she actually lives in Michigan (MCL 558.1, 558.21).

FOR WOMEN ONLY This Michigan law is based on the old English Common law. The companion Curtesy common law for men was abolished in Michigan, but a widower does have the right to an *elective share* to his wife's estate (see page 125).

 THERE COULD BE A LATER DEED

The above discussion on the different types of ownership of real property assumes that you are in possession of the most recent, valid Michigan deed. The decedent could have signed another, later, deed. Before you come to a conclusion about who inherits the property it is advisable have a title search done to determine the owner of the property as of the decedent's date of death.

OUT OF STATE DEED

The inheritance of real property located in the state of Michigan is determined by the laws of Michigan, and this is so regardless of whether the decedent was a resident of the state of Michigan. Similarly, if the decedent owned property in another state or country, then even if the decedent was a Michigan resident, the laws of the state or country where the property is located determine who inherits property in that state.

The laws of each state are similar, but not the same. In Michigan property held as Joint Tenants belongs to the surviving joint owner, but states differ in how the deed needs to be worded in order to have a right of survivorship. Many states require the deed specifically state that there are Rights Of Survivorship. In such states a deed held as Joint Tenants (and no stated Right of Survivorship) is the same as a Tenancy In Common.

If the decedent owned property in another state, then it is important to consult with an attorney in that state to determine who now owns the property.

PROPERTY HELD IN TRUST

BANK/ SECURITY ACCOUNTS

If a bank account is registered in the name of the decedent held "in trust for" or "for the benefit of" someone, then once the bank has a certified copy of the death certificate, the bank will turn over the account to the beneficiary. If the beneficiary is not yet 18, and the amount greater than $5,000, then the monies must be paid to the child's legally appointed guardian (MCL 487.702). See Chapter 9 for a discussion about appointing a guardian for a child.

If a bank or credit union account is registered in the name of the decedent "as Trustee under a Trust agreement," that means the decedent was the Trustee of a Trust and the bank will turn over that account to the Successor Trustee of the Trust. Banks usually require a copy of the Trust agreement when the account was opened, so the bank probably knows the identity of the Successor Trustee. If the Successor Trustee is deceased, then the monies go to the beneficiaries of the Trust. And if all of the beneficiaries are deceased, then the monies will become part of the decedent's Probate Estate (MCL 490.57).

MOTOR VEHICLE

If the motor vehicle is held in the name of the decedent "as Trustee," then the motor vehicle continues to be Trust property. The Successor Trustee will need to contact the motor vehicle bureau to have title changed to that of the Successor Trustee. If the Trust agreement directs the Successor Trustee to sell the car or to distribute that car to a beneficiary, then the Successor Trustee will need to arrange to have this done. See Chapter 6 for directions about how to transfer the car to a new owner.

REAL PROPERTY

If the decedent had a Trust and put real property that he owned into the Trust, then the deed may read something like this:

> JOHN ZAMORA and MARIA ZAMORA,
> his wife, whose address is
> 200 Main Street, Dearborn, Michigan
> conveys and warrants to
> JOHN ZAMORA, **Trustee of the**
> **JOHN ZAMORA TRUST AGREEMENT**
> DATED FEBRUARY 26, 2000,
> the following real property
>
> . . .

The death of the Trustee of a Trust does not change the ownership of the property. It remains in the Trust. The Trust document might say whether the person who takes John's place as Trustee (the Successor Trustee) should sell or keep the property or perhaps give it to a beneficiary. If no instruction is given, the Successor Trustee can use his discretion as to what to do with the property. His decision may be affected by laws relating to the administration of Trust property in the state where the property is located.

If you are a beneficiary of the Trust and you are concerned about what the Successor Trustee will do with the property, then it is best to consult with your attorney to learn about your rights under that Trust.

PROPERTY IN DECEDENT'S NAME ONLY

If the decedent owned property that was in his name only (not jointly or in trust for someone), then some sort of Probate procedure will be necessary before the heirs can get possession of that property. Who is entitled to the decedent's Probate Estate depends on whether the decedent died with or without a Will. If the decedent died *testate* (with a Will), then the beneficiaries of the decedent's property are identified in the Will.

If the decedent died intestate, then the state of Michigan provides a Will for him in the form of a set of Laws of Intestate Succession. These laws determine who inherits the decedent's intestate Probate Estate and what percentage of the Probate Estate each heir is to receive once all the bills and costs of administering the Probate procedure are paid.

The law recognizes the right of the family to inherit the decedent's property. The law covers all possible relationships beginning with the decedent's spouse.

Who Is The Spouse?
In this era of people challenging the concept of the family unit, those of a philosophical bent may ponder the meaning of marriage. Is it a union of two people in the eyes of God? Is it even a union? The state does not concern itself with such things. If a person dies without a Will, then the state will distribute the decedent's Probate Estate according to the laws of the state; and the laws of the state determine whether two people are married.

MARRIED IN MICHIGAN

Michigan defines a legal marriage as a civil contract between a man and woman (i.e., they promise to marry each other), followed by the couple obtaining a license and then participating in a state or religious ceremony (MCL 551.2).

Michigan law specifically prohibits the marriage of people:

- ☒ who are currently married;
- ☒ who are insane or idiots;
- ☒ who are the same sex;
- ☒ who are related closer than second cousin;
- ☒ who are related through marriage as follows:

a man cannot marry his stepmother or stepdaughter or his daughter-in-law (i.e., his son's former wife) or his grandson's former wife or his grandfather's former wife, his mother-in-law, his wife's grandmother, his wife's granddaughter. Similarly, a woman cannot marry her stepfather, stepson, former son-in-law, etc. (MCL 551.1, 551.3, 551.4, 551.5, 552.1).

THE COMMON LAW MARRIAGE

A common law marriage is one that has not been solemnized by ceremony. The couple agree to live together as man and wife, and then publicly hold themselves out as being married. Many states (including Michigan) no longer recognize a common law marriage as being valid, and have passed laws to that effect. With the exception of same sex marriages, Michigan respects the laws of other states (MCL 555.271, 551.272). A common law marriage that is valid in another state could be valid in Michigan as well. If it is found to be valid in Michigan, then the surviving spouse can inherit the decedent's property under Michigan's Laws of Intestate Succession.

It is important to consult with an attorney if you have any question about the validity of the decedent's marriage.

MICHIGAN'S INTESTATE LAWS

If the decedent died without a Will, then the state of Michigan provides one for him in the form of the Michigan Laws of Intestate Succession:

MARRIED, NO SURVIVING CHILD OR PARENT
If at the time of death the decedent was married and had no surviving *descendants* (children, grandchildren, great-grandchildren, etc.) and no surviving parent, then all of the decedent's Probate Estate goes to the surviving spouse (MCL 700.2102(a)).

MARRIED WITH CHILD
If the decedent had children, one or more with the surviving spouse, then the surviving spouse gets the first $150,000** and half of the balance of the estate. If the decedent had children, but none with the surviving spouse, then the spouse gets $100,000** and half the Probate Estate and the child(ren) get the other half (MCL 700.2101(b),(f)).

MARRIED WITH PARENT, NO CHILD
If the decedent was married, without any descendant, but one of his parents survive him, then the spouse gets the first $150,000** and 3/4ths of the balance of the Probate Estate. The parent(s) of the decedent get the remaining 1/4 (MCL 700.2102(c)).

** COST OF LIVING ADJUSTMENT
The values as set by statute are subject to cost of living increases. For those who die after December 31, 2000, the dollar amount will be multiplied by the cost-of-living adjustment as determined by the Michigan Department of the Treasury. The specific dollar amount will be rounded to the nearest $1,000. Each January, the Treasury will publish a cost of living adjustment for those who die during the year (MCL 700.1210).

CHILD, NO SPOUSE

If the decedent was single, with descendants, then they inherit his Probate Estate (MCL 700.2103(a))

NO CHILD, NO SPOUSE

If the decedent had no spouse or descendant, then his property is divided equally between his parents. If only one of his parents is alive, then all of the property goes to that parent. If neither parent is alive, then the estate goes to the decedent's brothers and sisters.

There is no distinction between full blood siblings or half blood siblings. For example, if the decedent had one brother with the same set of parents, and another brother with the same father and a different mother, then both brothers inherit an equal amount (MCL 700.2103(b), 700.2107).

If the decedent had no brothers, sisters, or any of their descendants (nephews, nieces, great nieces or nephews, etc.) then the Probate Estate is divided in half with half going to the decedent's maternal grandparents, or their descendants; and the other half going to his paternal grandparents, or their descendants (MCL 700.2103(d)).

THE STATE: HEIR OF LAST RESORT

If a person dies without a Will and he has absolutely no next of kin, then as a last resort, his property goes to the state of Michigan (MCL 700.2105).

INHERITING BY REPRESENTATION

If the decedent died intestate and had two or more children, all who survive him, then each children inherits an equal share of his estate. But suppose one of his children died before he did. What happens to the share intended for the deceased child?

The same question occurs with other relatives. Suppose the decedent was survived only by brothers and sisters, then each inherits an equal share of the estate. But suppose one of the brothers died before the decedent. What happens to the share intended for that sibling?

In such cases, the property is distributed *by representation*, which is defined by Michigan statute 700.2106 as follows:

If a decedent's estate passes **by representation**, then

> ". . . the estate or part of the estate is divided into as many equal shares as the total of the surviving descendants in the generation nearest to the decedent that contains 1 or more surviving descendants and the deceased descendants in the same generation who left surviving descendants, if any. Each surviving descendant in the nearest generation is allocated 1 share. The remaining shares, if any, are combined and then divided in the same manner among the surviving descendants of the deceased descendants as if the surviving descendants who were allocated a share and their surviving descendants had predeceased the decedent. "

If you understood the above definition and you are not a lawyer, then you missed your calling. For the rest of us (even lawyers) its a head-scratcher. Perhaps the best way to explain the term is by example.

ALL CHILDREN SURVIVE
Suppose the decedent was unmarried with 4 children, Ann, Barry, Carl, David and he dies intestate, then each of his children get 25% of his estate.

CHILD WITHOUT DESCENDANTS DIES BEFORE DECEDENT
If Ann dies before her father leaving no descendants, then Barry, Carl and David divide the estate between them and each gets one third.

CHILDREN WITH DESCENDANTS DIES BEFORE DECEDENT
Suppose instead that only Carl and David survived their father. If Ann died leaving 2 children and Barry died leaving 3 children, then the estate is divided into 4 shares — one for each surviving child and one share for each deceased child who left descendants. Carl and David each get their 25% share. The other 50% of the estate is divided equally among the five grandchildren; i.e., each will get $1/10^{th}$ of the intestate estate.

CAUTION IT ISN'T ALL THAT SIMPLE

The explanation in this book of the Laws of Intestate Succession is abridged. Even though you may now know more about Michigan Intestate Succession than you ever wanted to know, there is much more to the law. For example, we did not explain in detail exactly how the estate is distributed if the decedent is survived only by descendants of his maternal or paternal grandparents. We could give an example explaining the law, but we thought you might enjoy a puzzle instead:

Winston died intestate leaving $100,000. His only relatives were his Aunt Susie, on his mother's side, and her two children Ramona and Abigail; and a second cousin Elvis, on his father's side (i.e., the child of a deceased first cousin). How much does each relative receive?

(Hint: see the definition of "by representation")

You can check your answer by visiting the Michigan section of the Eagle Publishing Company Web site:
http://www.eaglepublishing.com

THE RIGHTS OF A CHILD

ADOPTED CHILD

An adopted child has the same rights to inherit property from his adoptive parents as does a natural child. Whether the adoptive child can inherit from his natural parents depends on the circumstances of the adoption. If one of the child's parents dies, and the child is later adopted by a stepparent, then that child still retains full rights of inheritance from both of his natural parents, and their respective families. But if a Court terminates the rights of his natural parent(s), then that includes the right to inherit property (MCL 700.2114, 710.60).

AFTERBORN CHILD

If a child was conceived prior to the decedent's death, and born after the death, then the child inherits the same as any other natural child of the decedent (MCL 700.2108).

NON-MARITAL CHILD

A child born out of wedlock has the same rights to inherit from his/her natural father as does one born in wedlock, provided:

☑ the decedent and the natural mother of the child signed a document called an Acknowledgment of Parentage

— or —

☑ paternity was established by a court of law in this or any other state (MCL 722.712, 722.714, 722.1003)

If the decedent denied his paternity, then it will take a court procedure to establish (or disprove) paternity. If you want to establish paternity, then you need to consult with an attorney who is experienced in litigation. If DNA tests need to be conducted, and the family plans to cremate the decedent, you may need to have your attorney move quickly to bar cremation until the matter is settled.

THE CHILD OF AN ASSISTED CONCEPTION

Medical technology has made important contributions to solving the problem of infertility. There are all sorts of solutions, from hormone replacement therapy, to sperm banks that provide donations anonymously, to frozen sperm and/or ova to be thawed and used at a later date, to women who become a surrogate or gestation mother.

Solving a set of medical problems has opened the door to a new set of legal problems. Used to be, the only question was "Who's the father?" Now it could well be "Who's the mother? Two major problems are the case of a woman who has an assisted conception without the knowledge and/or consent of her spouse; and the case of a child that was born to a surrogate mother.

Under Michigan law, if a child is born to parents using any form of assisted conception, then that child has the same rights as a child born the old fashioned way. It is presumed that the father consented to the procedure. If it happens that the husband is not the father of the child or did not consent to assisted conception, then the husband can petition the court to terminate his parental rights and responsibilities. If the husband is successful the child will not be able to inherit from the husband, nor his family.

Some states, such as Virginia, allow a couple to contract with a woman to have their baby. The court supervises the contract and then issues a birth certificate to the intended parents after the birth. This is not the case in Michigan. Surrogate parent contracts are strictly prohibited in Michigan. Anyone who arranges or participates in such a contract can be found guilty of a felony that is punishable by a fine up to $50,000 and up to 5 years in jail, or both (MCL 700.2114, 722.855, 722.857).

WHO DIED FIRST?

Michigan statute requires that an heir survive the decedent by at least 120 hours (5 days) in order to inherit property according to the Michigan's Laws of Intestate Succession. If an heir does not live for at least 5 days after the decedent's death, then the decedent's property is distributed as if the heir died first. This rule also applies to property inherited by Will, unless the Will makes some different provision. The rule does not apply if it would result in the state of Michigan taking the property (MCL 700.2104, 700.2702).

Sometimes it happens that two family members die simultaneously, and no one knows who died first. For example, suppose a father and son die together in a car crash, how is the property distributed in that case?

Michigan statute provides for an orderly distribution of their respective estates. Each person is assumed to have survived the other and the property of each is distributed on that basis. The father's property is distributed as if he survived his son and the son's property is distributed as if he survived his father. For example, if the father had a $10,000 insurance policy with his son as beneficiary and his daughter as alternate beneficiary, then the money will go to his daughter.

If the father and son owned property jointly, then if they die simultaneously, the property is divided with one half going to the estate of the father and the other half to the estate of his son.

Special Situation

NO SHARE FOR KILLER

Anyone convicted in a civil suit or a criminal suit of intentionally causing the death of the decedent, is prohibited from profiting from the crime. Property that the killer (or his accomplice) would have inherited as a beneficiary of the decedent's Will or according to the Michigan Laws of Intestate Succession, will be distributed as if the killer (and accomplice) died before the decedent.

If the killer, or accomplice, is a beneficiary of a life insurance policy, then whoever is named as alternate beneficiary will get the insurance proceeds. If the killer (or accomplice) is a joint tenant with the decedent, then he/she loses all of rights of survivorship (MCL 700.2803).

☎ LAWYER

NO SHARE FOR NEGLECTFUL PARENT

Any parent who has not openly treated the child as his or hers and who has neglected to support their minor child is barred from inheriting property from that minor child under the Laws of Intestate Succession. The Probate court is not going to deny a parent's inheritance unless evidence is presented that the parent in effect abandoned the minor child. If you believe that a parent is not entitled to inherit the decedent's property on any of the above grounds, then you need to employ an attorney experienced in Probate litigation to present such evidence to the Probate Court (MCL 700.2114).

WHEN TO CHALLENGE THE WILL

It is not uncommon for a family member to be unhappy with the way the decedent willed his property. If you are tempted to challenge a Will, first consider whether the Will is valid under Michigan law.

In Michigan, a Will is presumed to be valid if at the time the decedent made the Will:

➢ he was at least 18 years of age

➢ he was of sound mind

The decedent is thought to have acted with sound mind if:

☑ he knew what he was doing (namely making a Will);

☑ he knew what property he had;

☑ he remembered and understood his relationship to his family members and how they would be affected by his Will;

☑ he was not suffering from a delusional mental disorder affecting his ability to distribute his property;

Michigan statute requires that the Will be in writing and signed by the person who is making the Will in the presence of two witnesses (MCL 700. 2501, 700.2502).

THE UNWITNESSED WILL

The first step in the Probate procedure is to have the Probate court determine whether the Will presented is valid. If the Will is in writing and signed by the Will maker in the presence of at least two credible witnesses, then there should be no problem in having the Will accepted into Probate. But suppose the decedent wrote out a Will in his own hand and signed it with no one present? Such a Will is called a *holographic Will.* Many states refuse to accept a holographic Will into Probate. But in Michigan, the Probate Court will accept a holographic Will, provided it is dated, and signed by the decedent, and the material (important) parts of the Will were handwritten by the decedent (MCL 700.2502).

The problem with a holographic Will, in this or any other state, is its authenticity. Because no one saw the decedent sign the Will, it is hard to determine whether the Will was written by the decedent or is a forgery.

If all the decedent left was a holographic Will, then you need to consult with an attorney experienced in Probate matters, to present evidence to the court that the Will does (or does not) qualify as a holographic Will in the state of Michigan.

THE VERBAL WILL

Picture a death bed scene. The elderly gentleman is surrounded by several family members. In a whisper, just audible enough to be heard, he says:

"Even though I am a wealthy man, I never got around to making a Will. You all have been good to me, but I did want my entire fortune to go to my nephew, Robert. He has been like a son to me. "

Do you think Robert can inherit his Uncle's estate?

Not in Michigan unless:
- ⇨ Someone writes down his uncles's wishes, and
- ⇨ The uncle acknowledges that this is his Will, and
- ⇨ The uncle tells someone to sign the Will for him, and
- ⇨ The person does so, and two people sign the Will as witnesses (MCL 700.2502).

Considering that the uncle's relatives will probably inherit the fortune under the Michigan's Laws of Intestate Succession, it is doubtful that Robert is in danger of becoming wealthy at any time in the near future.

THE WILL THAT IS CONTRARY TO LAW

Sometimes a person who is of sound mind, makes a Will, but that Will has the effect of giving a spouse or a minor child less than is required under Michigan law. One such example is that of Nancy. Hers was not an easy life. She worked long hours as a waitress. She divorced her hard drinking first husband. The final judgment gave her their homestead, some securities, and sole custody of their son. After the divorce Nancy had her attorney prepare a Will leaving all she owned to her son, Richard.

Some years later she met and married Harry, a chef at the restaurant where she worked. He moved into her home and they later had twin girls. Richard was 19, and his stepsisters 12, when Nancy died after a lengthy battle with cancer.

Nancy did not leave much — her car, her home, cash and securities worth about $50,000, all of which was in her name only.

Before she died, she told Richard, that she had not changed her Will because she wanted him to have all she owned. She said Harry had a good job and she was sure he would take good care of his daughters.

No sooner was the funeral over, when stepson came in and demanded that Harry vacate his mother's home. Harry was furious and went to his attorney.

"I was a good husband to Nancy, supporting and taking care of her all during her illness. It was me, and not her son, who was at her side when she died. Don't I have any rights? And how about the twins. Don't they have any rights?"

The attorney explained "The twins were born after your wife made her Will, so Michigan statute 700.2302 gives them the right to inherit as much as their stepbrother. Unless your wife made some separate provision for the twins, all three children will inherit an equal share of their mother's estate. "

"No, Nancy did not make any provision for the twins."

The attorney continued "You also have rights in Nancy's Probate Estate provided you did not give up those rights. Michigan statute 700.2205 allows you to waive your rights by signing a pre-nuptial or post-nuptial agreement. Did you sign any such document?"

"Absolutely not!"

"In that case, you are entitled to a Homestead Allowance of $15,000; and up to $18,000 as a Family Allowance to support you and the twins during the Probate procedure, plus you are entitled to up to Exempt property, i.e., up to $10,000 in value of her car or home furnishings."

"But what about the house? That's worth the most amount of money. Don't I have Dower rights or something?

The attorney explained "Dower rights are for Widows. Curtesy rights are for men, but they don't have Curtesy rights here in Michigan. You do have the right to ask the Court for an *elective share* of your wife's estate. In Michigan, instead of agreeing to what you will receive under the Will (which in your case is nothing) you can elect take half of what you would have received if she died without a Will and that amount is reduced by half the value of anything you received because of her death. That includes the proceeds of a life insurance policy, or any property that you held as husband and wife, or any gift she made to you that exceeded $10,000 in value in any given year for the two years before she died.

"No she didn't give me anything, there was no insurance and we didn't own property together."

"In that case you can elect to take the first $75,000, and twenty five percent of whatever is left."

"Sound's good to me. I'll take $15,000 Homestead Allowance, the $18,000 Family Allowance, the car is worth $10,000 so I'll take it as Exempt Property. I'll take the $75,000 and one quarter of what's ever left. And since each child is entitled, to an equal share, that means Richard is entitled to only one quarter of whatever is left.

"Not so fast. All of this is subject to court approval. Once an inventory is taken, and the creditors have had a chance to present their claims, you have 63 days to file your election with the Probate court." (MCL 700.2201, 700.2202).

Richard did not fare as well as his mother intended. There was no cash left in the estate after the funeral expenses, medical bills, the Homestead and Family Allowances, and the costs of probating the estate were paid. All that Richard inherited was his fractional share of the house. And he didn't get that until his stepfather moved out at the end of the year.

No doubt Nancy did not understand what would happen to her estate once she passed on. The Will she left did not accomplish her goal of providing for her son. All it did was cause turmoil and an irreparable rift between Harry and Richard. It didn't need to be that way. Had Nancy known about Michigan law, she could have consulted with an attorney and set up an estate plan that could have provided for her son, without alienating her husband.

But, the moral of the story, for the purpose of this discussion, is that if you believe that the decedent's Will is not valid or is not drafted according to Michigan law, then you need to consult with an attorney experienced in Probate matters to determine your legal rights under that Will.

Getting Possession Of The Property

Knowing who is entitled to receive the decedent's property is one thing. Getting that property is another. As explained in the previous chapter if the decedent held property jointly with someone, or in a trust for someone, the property now belongs to the joint owner or beneficiary. If it is personal property such as a bank account or a security, the beneficiary can usually get possession of the property by giving a certified copy of the death certificate to the financial institution.

If the decedent had real or personal property in his name only, or if he held property as a tenant-in-common, then some sort of Probate procedure may be necessary in order to transfer ownership to the proper beneficiary. In most cases a full Probate procedure is necessary and that will require the assistance of an attorney, but there are a few items that can be transferred without legal assistance. This chapter explains how to get possession of these items. The chapter also contains an explanation of the different kinds of Probate procedures and when it is appropriate to use that procedure.

DISTRIBUTING PERSONAL PROPERTY

Too often, the first person to discover the body will help himself to the decedent's *personal property* (clothing, jewelry, appliances, electrical equipment, cameras, books, household items and furnishing, etc.). Unless that person is the decedent's sole beneficiary, such action is unconscionable, if not illegal.

If the decedent was married and did not have children, then all of the decedent's personal effects belong to his spouse unless he left a Will giving a particular item of personal property to someone else. The decedent may have left a separate writing leaving some personal item to a particular beneficiary. Under Michigan law, a person can leave any of his personal effects (not money) by means of a separate writing. To be distributed as part of a Probate procedure, the writing needs to be in the decedent's own hand or if the gift was made by means of a typewritten statement, then the decedent's signature needs to appear at the end of the document (MCL 700.2513). If no Probate procedure is necessary, then the item can just be given to the beneficiary.

If the decedent was not married, then his personal effects should be given to the person appointed as the Personal Representative. The Representative has the duty to distribute the property according to the decedent's Will, or separate writing, or according to the Michigan Laws of Intestate Succession in case the decedent died without a Will.

If you determine that there is no need for a Probate procedure and the decedent did not have a Will then his next of kin need to divide all of the personal effects among themselves in approximately equal proportions.

What's Equal?

The decedent's Will or if no Will, then the Michigan Laws of Intestate Succession may direct that the decedent's personal property be divided equally between two or more beneficiaries. The problem with the term "equal" is that people have different ideas of what "equal" means. Unless there is clear evidence that the decedent's Will meant something else, "equal" refers to the monetary value of the item and not to the number of items received. For example, to divide the decedent's personal effects equally, one beneficiary may receive an expensive item of jewelry and another beneficiary may receive several items whose overall value is approximately equal to that single piece of jewelry.

When distributing personal effects there needs to be cooperation and perhaps compromise, or else bitter arguments might arise over items of little monetary value. One such argument occurred when an elderly woman died who was rich only in her love for her five children and 12 grandchildren. After the funeral, the children gathered in their mother's apartment. Each child had his/her own furnishings and no need for anything in the apartment. They agreed to donate all of their mother's personal effects to a local charity with the exception of a few items of sentimental value.

Each child took some small item as a remembrance — a handkerchief, a large platter that their mother used to serve family dinners, a doily their mother crocheted. Things went smoothly until it came to her photograph album. Frank, the youngest sibling, said, "I'll take this." Marie objected saying, "But there are pictures in that album that I want."

Frank retorted, "You already took all the pictures Mom had on her dresser."

The argument went downhill from there. Unsettled sibling rivalries boiled over, fueled by the hurt of the loss that they were all experiencing.

It almost came to blows when the eldest settled the argument: "Frank you make copies of all of the photos in the album for Marie. Marie, you make copies of all of the pictures that you took and give them to Frank. This way you both will have a complete set of Mom's pictures. And while you're at it, make copies for the rest of us."

DELIVERY OF CASH UNDER $500

A hospital, convalescent or nursing home, morgue or law enforcement agency may turn over the decedent's wearing apparel, and up to $500 in cash to the decedent's spouse, child, or parent. The family member will need to furnish identification and sign a sworn statement that there is no pending Probate procedure.

Whoever takes the property has the duty to turn it over to whoever is entitled to that property. Cash must be distributed according to the decedent's Will or according to the Laws of Intestate Succession. If the decedent's Will contains a gift of personal property, then the person taking possession of an item mentioned in the Will has the legal (if not moral) responsibility to see that gift is distributed as the decedent wished (MCL 700.3981).

TRANSFERRING THE CAR

If the decedent owned a motor vehicle in his name only, then title to the car needs to be transferred to the new owner. The new owner needs to register the car in the state where it will be driven. You may want to limit the use of the car until it is transferred to the beneficiary. If the decedent's car is involved in an accident before the car is transferred to the new owner, then the decedent's estate may be liable for the damage. Having adequate insurance on the car may save the estate from monetary loss, but a pending lawsuit could delay Probate and prevent any money from being distributed to the beneficiaries until the lawsuit is settled.

If there is a Probate procedure then it is the Personal Representative's job to transfer the motor vehicles to the proper beneficiary. If the decedent had a Will and he made a specific gift of the car to someone, then the Personal Representative will transfer the car to that person. If the decedent was survived by a spouse, then the Court could award the car to the spouse as part of the Homestead Allowance (see page 91).

If there was no mention of the car in his Will, and the car is not included as part of the Homestead Allowance, then the car goes to the *residuary beneficiaries* under the Will, i.e., those who inherit whatever is left once all the bills have been paid and all the special gifts made in the Will are distributed.

If the decedent did not have a Will, then the car goes to the decedent's heirs as determined by the Michigan's Laws of Intestate Succession (see page 111).

TRANSFER WHEN MORE THAN ONE BENEFICIARY

If there is more than one person who has the right to inherit the car, then they all can take title to the car. That may not be a practical thing to do since only one person can drive the car at any given time and if one gets into an accident, then they all can be held liable. The better route is for the beneficiaries to agree to have one person take title to the car. The person taking title will need to compensate the others for their share of the car. In such case the beneficiaries need to come to an agreement as to the value of the car.

DETERMINING THE VALUE OF THE CAR

Cars are valued in many different ways. The *collateral* value of the car is the value that banks use to evaluate the car for purposes of making a loan to the owner of the car. Because banks print these values in book form, the collateral value is also referred to as the *book value* of the car. If you were to trade in a car for the purpose of purchasing a new car, then the car dealer will offer you the *wholesale* value of the car. Were you to purchase that same car from a car dealer, then he will price it at its *retail* or *fair market value*. Usually the retail price is highest, wholesale is lowest and the book value of the car is somewhere in between.

You can call your local bank to get the book value of the car. It may be more difficult to obtain the wholesale value of the car because the amount of money a dealer is willing to pay for the car depends on the value of the new car that you are purchasing. You can determine the car's retail value by looking at comparable used car advertisements in the local newspaper or over the Internet.

No Probate procedure is necessary to transfer motor vehicles owned by the decedent provided the total value of his motor vehicles is not greater than $60,000. If the value of the motor vehicles exceeds $60,000, or if there needs to be a Probate procedure, then the Personal Representative will make the transfer (MCL 257.234, 257.236).

Making the transfer is not difficult. All you need do is go to your local Michigan Secretary of State Branch Office with a certified copy of the death certificate. You can call the Michigan Secretary of State to determine the location of the nearest office at (517) 322-1166, or you can visit their Web site for the location of the branch nearest you:

 MICHIGAN DEPT. OF STATE DRIVER & VEHICLE
http://www.sos.state.mi.us

To make the transfer you will need to complete form TR-29 and turn in the last certificate of title. The Branch Office will give you the necessary form and assist you if you cannot locate the original certificate of title. Odometer statements are required to transfer cars that are built within 10 years of the date of transfer, so you may need to take a reading before you transfer the car. It is a good idea to first call your local Branch Office to determine the current transfer fee and whether there is any other information they may require.

You need to transfer the car registration at the same time you transfer title to the car. If the car is to remain in Michigan, then the new owner needs to produce proof of insurance. If the car is going to be transferred out of state, then the Michigan registration needs to be cancelled. It is also a good idea to cancel the decedent's driver's license at the same time and have his name deleted from the Secretary of State's mailing list.

TRANSFERRING WATERCRAFT AND SNOWMOBILES

In Michigan, a watercraft that is 20 feet or more in length with a permanently affixed engine needs to be titled and registered. If the decedent owned such a watercraft, then the title and registration certificates need to be transferred in the same manner as a motor vehicle. If the decedent owned a snowmobile, then its title and registration need to transferred as well. You can call your local Branch Office for information about making the transfer of a watercraft or snowmobile or visit the Michigan Secretary of State Web site (see page 133 for the site).

TRANSFERRING THE MOBILE HOME

The Secretary of State issues title certificates to Mobile Homes. Transfers are made much the same as a motor vehicle. You will need to go to the nearest Branch Office with a certified copy of the death certificate. You may want to first call and ask what other information they may require.

Before transferring the motor vehicle, you need to find out whether the land on which the mobile home is located was leased or owned by the decedent.

If the decedent was renting space in a trailer park, then you need to contact the trailer park owner to transfer the lease agreement to the beneficiary of the mobile home. If the decedent owned the land under the mobile home, then a Probate procedure will be necessary to transfer the land to the proper beneficiary. See page 141 for information about transferring real property.

The leased car is not an asset of the estate because the decedent did not own the car. The leased car is a liability to the estate because the decedent was obligated to pay the balance of the monies owed on the lease agreement. The Personal Representative, or next of kin, needs to work out an agreement with the company to either assign the lease to a beneficiary or family member who will agree to pay for the lease, or to have the estate pay off the lease by purchasing the car under the terms of the lease agreement.

Some lenders will allow the lease to be assigned to a beneficiary provided the estate remains liable for the balance of payment. In such cases, it is better to have the beneficiary refinance the car and have the original lease agreement paid in full.

If the remaining payments exceed the current market value of the car, there may be a temptation to hand the keys over to the leasing company. This may not be the best strategy, because the leasing company can sell the car and then sue the estate for the balance of the monies owed. If the decedent had no assets or if the only assets he had are creditor proof, then simply returning the car may be an option. But if the decedent's estate has assets available to pay the balance of the lease payments, then the Personal Representative needs to arrange to have the car transferred in a way that releases the estate from all further liability.

INCOME TAX REFUNDS

Any refund due to the decedent under a joint federal income tax return filed by his surviving spouse will be sent to the surviving spouse. If the decedent's Personal Representative filed the final return, then the refund check will be sent to him to be deposited to the estate account.

If the decedent was single and no Probate procedure is necessary, then whoever is entitled to the decedent's estate is entitled to the refund check. If you are the beneficiary of the decedent's estate, you can obtain the refund by filing IRS form 1310 along with the decedent's final income tax return (the 1040). You can obtain form 1310 from the decedent's accountant, or if he did not have an accountant and you wish to file yourself, you can call the IRS at (800) 829-3676 to obtain the form. You can get instructions, publications and forms from the Internal Revenue Service Web site:

IRS WEB SITE
IRS FORMS AND INSTRUCTIONS
http://www.irs.ustreas.gov/prod/forms_pubs/forms.html
IRS PUBLICATIONS
http://www.irs.ustreas.gov/prod/forms_pubs/pubs.html

The Personal Representative does not need to file form 1310 because once he files the decedent's final income tax return, any refund will be forwarded to him. Similarly, it is not necessary for the surviving spouse who filed a joint return to file form 1310.

THE STATE INCOME TAX REFUND

The decedent's final Michigan State income tax return needs to be filed at the same time the federal income tax return is filed. As with the federal return, the surviving spouse can file a joint return, and any state income tax refund will be distributed to the spouse. If there is no surviving spouse, then the Personal Representative needs to file the final state income tax return. Any refund will be sent to the Personal Representative to be deposited to the estate account.

If no Probate procedure is necessary, and you filed form 1310 with the IRS, then you can mail a copy of that form to the Michigan Department of Treasury to receive any Michigan Income Tax refund that may be due:

MICHIGAN DEPARTMENT OF TREASURY

430 West Allegan Street

Lansing, MI 48922

If no federal income tax is due, then Michigan Tax form MI 1310 must be filed with the Michigan Department of Treasury. You can obtain the form by calling (800) 827-4000 or you can download the form from the Michigan Treasury Web site:

 MICHIGAN DEPARTMENT OF TREASURY
http://www.treasury.state.mi.us

Only a Personal Representative can file form MI 1310. If the decedent's estate does not exceed $15,000, you may be able to have a Personal Representative appointed and then use an abridged Probate procedure as described later in this chapter.

THE SMALL ESTATE

Suppose that the decedent had his affairs arranged so that the only thing he had in his name was a stock certificate. If the value of the stock does not exceed $15,000, plus the cost of living adjustment ("COLA") as determined by the Michigan Department of Treasury (and described in Chapter 4), then whoever is entitled to inherit the property can do so by giving the company who issued the stock a sworn written statement (an *Affidavit*) that the following facts are true:

☑ The decedent's estate does not include real property and the value of his entire estate (not including monies owed on the property) does not exceed $15,000 plus the COLA.

☑ 28 days have passed since the decedent's death.

☑ No one has applied to be appointed as Personal Representative.

☑ The name and address of each person entitled to the property is stated and the person signing the document is entitled to receive the property.

The State Court Administrative Office has a standard form (PC 598) that you can use to present to whoever has possession of the decedent's property (MCL 700.3983). You can pick up the form from the Register at the Probate Court in your county.

Under Michigan law, whoever transfers the decedent's property under an Affidavit, is released from liability just the same as if he transferred it to the decedent's Personal Representative (MCL 700.3984). Still a person may hesitate to make the transfer without a Court order. If such is the case, then whoever is entitled to receive the property can go to Court and obtain a Court order using the procedure described on the next page.

COURT ORDER TO DISTRIBUTE SMALL ESTATES

If the decedent died without a Will, then under Michigan law, the Probate Court can issue an order that real or personal property held in the decedent's name only, be transferred to his surviving spouse; or if none, then who ever is entitled to the property under Michigan's Intestate Laws. The Court will issue the order without the need for any Probate procedure, provided that after funeral and burial expenses have been paid, the decedent's estate is not greater than $15,000 (plus COLA).

Before issuing the order, the Court will require proof that the funeral and burial expenses have been paid. If these bills have not been paid, then the order will require the funeral and burial expenses be paid, and whatever remains, given to the surviving spouse or whoever is entitled to inherit the property.

Because of the Homestead Allowance, the spouse or the decedent's minor child or dependent child are entitled to receive the property free of creditor claims (see Page 91). Anyone else who inherits the property, must use that property to pay anyone who makes a valid claim for those funds within 63 days of the date of the order (MCL 700.3982).

If the decedent died with a Will or the amount to be transferred is more than $15,000 + COLA + funeral + burial expenses, then the Court will require that a Personal Representative be appointed, and a Probate procedure be conducted. If there are few assets to be distributed, then it may be appropriate to use a shortened procedure called Summary Administration. This procedure is described on the next page.

SUMMARY ADMINISTRATION

There is no need to go through the full Probate procedure if there are few or no assets that can be distributed to the beneficiary. Why notify creditors if there is no money to pay claims? As explained on page 91, there is a priority of payment. No creditor can be paid until the following items are satisfied:

⇨ costs and expenses of administration including attorney and Personal Representative fees.

⇨ reasonable funeral and burial expenses

⇨ homestead allowance ($15,000)

⇨ family allowance ($18,000)

⇨ exempt property ($10,000)

⇨ federal taxes with priority

⇨ reasonable medical and hospital expenses of the decedent's last illness.

If the inventory shows that no money will be left after paying for the above, then the Personal Representative can immediately disburse the funds in the above order and then close out the estate. This abridged Probate procedure is called *Summary Administration* (MCL 700.3987).

TRANSFERRING REAL PROPERTY

As explained in Chapter 5, no Probate procedure is necessary to transfer real property if the decedent held that property:

⇨   as the owner of a life estate   — or —

⇨   jointly with rights of survivorship   — or —

⇨   with his spouse as tenants by the entirety.

The surviving joint owner(s) owns the property as of the date of death, however, the decedent's name remains on the deed. Anyone examining title to the property will not know of the death unless the decedent's death certificate is recorded with the Register of Deeds in the county where the property is located (MCL 565.48). The reason this is necessary is because the Michigan Vital Records Office is responsible only for issuing the death certificate. They do not publish the document, so it is not part of the public record.

It is not necessary to have the death certificate recorded until you transfer the property. But that may be years in the future and you may have long since misplaced the death certificate. To save yourself the hassle of obtaining a death certificate at a later date, you may want to have it recorded at this time. To do so you can call the Register of Deeds in the county where the property is located and ask where to mail the death certificate and how much money you should send for the recording fee.

You should enclose a self addressed stamped envelop for the Register to return the recorded death certificate to you once it is recorded. You may want to keep the recorded death certificate together with the deed to the property so you will have a record of the book and page in which the death certificate was recorded.

If the decedent held real property in his name only or jointly with another as Tenants in Common, then a Probate procedure is necessary. The type procedure depends on the value of the property. If the decedent died without a Will and property is not worth more than $15,000 (plus COLA, plus funeral and burial expenses), you may be able to have it transferred to the proper beneficiary by means of a Court order as described on Page 139. If that is not an option then a Personal Representative will need to be appointed in order to transfer the property to the proper beneficiary.

The attorney for the Personal Representative will arrange to have the decedent's real property transferred and will have documents recorded that identify the new owner. If you are the new owner, you should receive all of the original recorded documents to keep for your records.

 **LAWYER**   TRANSFERRING
OUT OF STATE PROPERTY

Each state regulates the transfer of real property within that state. Some states, such as Florida, have rules much like Michigan, i.e., the death certificate is recorded to notify people examining title to the property that the Grantee is now deceased. Other states, such as Ohio, require an Affidavit of Survivorship or a Certificate of Transfer to be recorded. If the decedent owned property in another state, then it is important to contact an attorney in that state to find out what documents need to be recorded at this time.

THE FULL PROBATE PROCEDURE

There will need to be a full Probate procedure if the decedent left a Will and there is property that cannot be transferred using any of the procedures previously discussed in this chapter.

A full Probate procedure is a fairly complex process. It can take anywhere from several months to more than a year depending on the size and complexity of the Probate Estate. It is the Personal Representative's job to use the Probate Estate to pay all valid claims and then to distribute what is left to the proper beneficiary.

All of the decedent's debts are paid from the Probate Estate and not from the Personal Representative's pocket; but if the Personal Representative makes a mistake then he may be responsible to pay for that mistake. For example, the Personal Representative is personally liable if he distributes the estate to the beneficiaries and has not paid sufficient state taxes (MCL 205.244). In such case the required taxes will come out of his own pocket, unless he can convince the beneficiaries to contribute the required sum.

The Personal Representative needs to employ an attorney to guide him through the process. It then becomes the job of the attorney for the Personal Representative to see to it that the estate is administered properly and without any personal liability to the Representative.

If you are the Personal Representative, then your attorney will explain all the things that need to be done, and will prepare all of the documents that need to be filed with the Court.

YOUR RIGHTS AS A BENEFICIARY

The Probate Court is in charge of supervising the Probate procedure, however, much of the Personal Representative's job is done independently and without seeking permission from the Probate Court. If you are a beneficiary if the decedent's estate, then it is important that you know what rights you have and where necessary to assert those rights.

✧ RIGHT TO YOUR OWN ATTORNEY

The attorney who handles the estate is employed by, and represents, the Personal Representative. If the estate is sizeable, consider employing your own attorney to check that things are done properly and in a timely manner. Even with a small estate, you may want to consult with an attorney if at any time you are concerned about the way the Probate is being conducted.

✧ RIGHT TO APPROVE PERSONAL REPRESENTATIVE

Michigan statute 700.3203 gives an order of priority in the appointment of Personal Representative. Whoever the decedent named as Personal Representative in his Will has top priority. If that person is unable or unwilling to serve, then the surviving spouse can serve provided the spouse is also a beneficiary of the Will. If not then any beneficiary of the Will can serve as Personal Representative.

If the decedent died without a Will, then his spouse has the right to be appointed as Personal Representative. If there is no surviving spouse, or if the spouse is unable or unwilling to serve, then anyone who is a beneficiary of the estate can serve. If no one volunteers for the job, then after 42 days from the date of death, a creditor of the estate can have someone appointed to serve as Personal Representative.

You should receive notice that a Personal Representative has been appointed to administer the estate no later than a month after his appointment (MCL 700.3306, 700.3705). If someone wants to be Personal Representative and there are others with the same or a higher priority, then before being appointed that person must notify everyone with the same or higher priority that he will seek the appointment (MCL 700.3310).

If you have an objection to the person being appointed, then you need to let the Court know of your objection as soon as you learn of the intended appointment. You have the right to go before the Court on your own, but before doing so, you should consult with a Probate attorney. An experienced attorney will know what arguments will sway the Court, and what arguments will fail. The attorney can explain the best way for you to present your concerns to the Court.

✧ RIGHT TO ASK FOR COURT SUPERVISION

A Personal Representative can locate estate assets, pay bills, prepare an inventory, etc. all without the Court supervision. If you are concerned that monies from the estate are not being properly managed, or if you are concerned about the way the Personal Representative will distribute the estate property then you can file a Petition requesting that the Court supervise the procedure. Whether the Court grants your Petition depends on the circumstances of the case. If the decedent's Will requested an unsupervised administration, then the Court will not do so unless it is necessary for the protection of the people involved (MCL 700.3502).

If you want to ask for Court supervision, then it is advisable to seek the counsel of an attorney to help to prepare the Petition and present it to the Court.

✧ RIGHT TO DEMAND SUFFICIENT BOND

It doesn't happen often, but every now and again a Personal Representative will run off with estate funds. A bond is insurance for the estate. If estate property is stolen then the company that issued the bond will reimburse the estate for the loss. The Court will not order a bond unless the Court has some special concern or unless the Will specifically requires that the Personal Representative be bonded (MCL 700.3603). Most Wills state that no bond shall be required. The reason for omitting a bond is two-fold. The Will maker chooses someone he trusts to administer the estate, so he does not think a bond is necessary. And there are economic reasons. The cost of the bond is paid for by the estate, and ultimately the amount inherited is reduced by the amount paid for the bond.

Of course, the cost of the bond is not a factor, if you are concerned about insuring the estate from loss. Michigan statute 700.3605 gives any beneficiary of the estate who stands to inherit at least $2,500, or any creditor of the estate who has a claim in excess of $2,500 the right to make written demand for a bond. The written demand must be filed with the Register of the Probate Court, and if someone has been appointed as Personal Representative, then a copy of the demand must be mailed to him. The Personal Representative then has 28 days to obtain the bond and he is limited in his ability to administer the estate until he obtains the bond.

✧ RIGHT TO COPY OF INVENTORY

The Personal Representative must prepare an inventory of all of the assets of the Probate estate within 91 days of his appointment. He is required to send a copy of the inventory to each beneficiary of the estate and to any interested party (such as a creditor) who requests it. If you are not satisfied with the value assigned to any item, you have the right to ask the Court to supervise the administration and to appoint an appraiser to determine the clear market value of the item. The cost of the appraisal is a charge to the Probate estate; and the outcome of an appraisal can have tax consequences, so before requesting an appraisal, it is important to consult with your attorney for the best course of action (MCL 205.211, 205.212, 700.3706).

✧ RIGHT TO AN ACCOUNTING

The Personal Representative can close out the estate any time after 5 months have elapsed from the time of his appointment. If an Estate Tax Return must be filed, then it will probably take more than a year before the Personal Representative receives tax clearance and can close out the estate. The beneficiaries are entitled to an annual accounting if it takes more than a year to settle the estate (MCL 700.3703).

Before closing the estate the Personal Representative must give the beneficiaries a full accounting (MCL 700.3954). The accounting should start with the inventory value of the estate and end with the amount presently on hand. If the estate has significant assets, you may want your own accountant to look over the accounting.

You may be asked to sign a waiver of your right to an accounting, but keep in mind that the accounting is for your benefit. There are few situations that justify you giving up your right to know how estate monies were spent.

✧ RIGHT TO KNOW THE ATTORNEY'S FEES

The Personal Representative has the right to employ an attorney to guide him through the procedure, and to have the attorney's fee paid with estate funds. You, as a beneficiary, have the right to know how much will be charged for his services. The Administrative Rules of the Probate Court require that within 14 days of the appointment of the Personal Representative, or the employment of an attorney (whichever is later), the attorney must send a copy of the fee agreement together with a notice saying that you have the right to object to the fees charged at any time during the proceeding, or up to 28 days after the filing of the closing statement (Administrative Rule 8.303, MCL 700.3721).

✧ RIGHT TO APPROVE FEES

The Personal Representative is entitled to a reasonable fee for administering the estate. If he is also a beneficiary of the estate he may decide not to take a fee and just take his inheritance. The reason may be economic. Any fee the Personal Representative takes is taxable as ordinary income, but monies inherited are not taxable to him as a beneficiary. Ask the Personal Representative to tell you, in writing, whether he intends to ask for a fee, and if so, how much.

There are no statutory guidelines for what is a "reasonable" fee for the Personal Representative or for his attorney. You could call different law firms and ask what they would charge to Probate an estate with similar assets, and that will give you some idea of the going rate. If after doing some "comparison shopping" you believe that either the Personal Representative's fee or his attorney's fee is not reasonable, you can petition the Court to set these fees. It is best to have an attorney assist with such petition (MCL 700.3719)

✦ RIGHT TO RECEIVE A DEBT FREE INHERITANCE

Once a beneficiary finally receives his inheritance, the last thing he wants to hear is that there is some unfinished business, or worse yet that monies need to be paid from the inheritance he received. But that is just what could happen if the Personal Representative distributes the money before all the creditors are paid. An unpaid creditor could sue the Personal Representative any time within 6 months of the filing of the closing statement, or a creditor could sue any beneficiary within one year of receiving his inheritance, or 3 years from the date of death, whichever is later (MCL 700.3956, 700.3957).

You can protect yourself from this unhappy situation by checking to see that the Personal Representative gives proper notice to all of the decedent's creditors, and then verifying that they were paid. You should ask to see a copy of all of the tax returns that were filed, and then verify that any monies that were due have been paid. Most importantly, you should not agree to having the estate closed if the closing statement shows that there are any outstanding debts that need to be paid.

You have 28 days from the date that the Personal Representative files the closing statement, to raise an objection. If you have any question or concern about how the estate was administered, then this is your opportunity to bring those concerns to the attention of the Court (MCL 700.3958, 700.3988).

IT'S YOUR RIGHT - DON'T BE INTIMIDATED

As a beneficiary, you have many legal rights, but you may feel uncomfortable asserting those rights with a friend or family member who is Personal Representative. Don't be. It's your money and your legal right to be kept informed. Be especially firm if the Personal Representative waves you off with:

"You've known me for years. Surely you trust me."

People who are trustworthy, don't ask to be trusted. They do what is right. The very fact that the Personal Representative is resisting, is a red flag. In such situation, you can explain that it is not a matter of trust, but a matter of what is your legal right.

At the same time, keep things in perspective. Your relationship with the Personal Representative may be more important to you than the money you inherit. The job of settling an estate can be complex and demanding. If the Personal Representative is getting the job done, then let him know that you appreciate his efforts.

THE CHECK LIST

We discussed many things that need to be done when someone dies in the state of Michigan. The next page contains a check list that you may find helpful should someone near to you die.

You can check those items that you need to do, and then cross them off the list once they are done. We made the list as comprehensive as possible, so many items may not apply in your case. In such case, you can cross them off the list or mark them *N/A* (not applicable).

Things to do

FUNERAL ARRANGEMENTS TO BE MADE
☐ AUTOPSY   ☐ ANATOMICAL GIFT
☐ DISPOSITION OF BODY OR ASHES

DEATH CERTIFICATE
☐ HAVE CERTIFICATE RECORDED
GIVE COPY TO: _____
_____

NOTICE OF DEATH
PEOPLE TO BE NOTIFIED _____

COMPANIES TO NOTIFY
☐ TELEPHONE COMPANY
    ☐ LOCAL CARRIER   ☐ LONG DISTANCE   ☐ CELLULAR
☐ NEWSPAPER (OBITUARY PRINTED)
☐ NEWSPAPER CANCELLED   ☐ deposit refund
☐ SOCIAL SECURITY
☐ INTERNET SERVER
☐ TELEVISION CABLE COMPANY
☐ POWER & LIGHT   ☐ deposit refund
☐ POST OFFICE
☐ OTHER UTILITIES (GAS, WATER)   ☐ deposit refund
☐ PENSION PLAN
☐ ANNUITY
☐ HEALTH INSURANCE COMPANY
☐ LIFE INSURANCE COMPANY
☐ HOME INSURANCE COMPANY
☐ MOTOR VEHICLE INSURANCE COMPANY
☐ CONDOMINIUM OR HOMEOWNER ASSOCIATION
☐ CANCEL SERVICE CONTRACT   ☐ deposit refund
☐ CREDIT CARD COMPANIES _____
    _____
    _____

Things to do

REMOVE DECEDENT AS BENEFICIARY OF:
- ☐ WILL   ☐ INSURANCE POLICY   ☐ PENSION PLAN
- ☐ BANK OR IRA ACCOUNT   ☐ SECURITY

DEBTS
PAY DECEDENT'S DEBTS (AMOUNT & CREDITOR)

_____

COLLECT MONIES OWED TO DECEDENT (AMOUNT & DEBTOR)

_____

TAXES
- ☐ FILE FINAL FEDERAL INCOME TAX RETURN
- ☐ FILE FINAL STATE INCOME TAX RETURN
- ☐ RECEIVE INCOME TAX REFUND
- ☐ FILE ESTATE TAX RETURN

PROPERTY TO BE TRANSFERRED
- ☐ PERSONAL EFFECTS
- ☐ MOTOR VEHICLE
- ☐ BANK ACCOUNT
- ☐ CREDIT UNION ACCOUNT
- ☐ IRA ACCOUNT
- ☐ SECURITIES
- ☐ BROKERAGE ACCOUNT
- ☐ INSURANCE PROCEEDS
- ☐ HOMESTEAD
- ☐ TIME SHARE
- ☐ OTHER REAL PROPERTY
- ☐ CONTENTS OF SAFE DEPOSIT BOX

OTHER THINGS TO DO

_____
_____
_____

Once the Probate procedure is over, you will be left with many documents and wonder which you need to keep:

COURT DOCUMENTS
You should keep a copy of the inventory to establish the value of property that you inherit. That value becomes your basis for any Capital Gains tax that you may need to pay in the future. Other than the inventory, there is no reason to keep any Court document, provided you are satisfied with the way things were done; and do not intend to take action against the Personal Representative, or his attorney. The Clerk of the Probate Court keeps the Probate file on record, so if for some reason you later need a copy of a Probate document, you can get it from the Clerk.

PERSONAL DOCUMENTS
You may wish to keep the decedent's personal papers (birth certificate, marriage certificate, naturalization papers, army records, religious documents, etc.) for your own personal records. You may want to keep the decedent's medical records in the event that a member of the family needs to check out a genetic disease.

TAX RECORDS
The IRS has up to three years to collect additional taxes, and you have up to 7 years to claim a loss from a worthless security, so you should keep the decedent's tax file for seven years from the date of filing the return. You can learn more about which records to keep from the IRS publication 552. You can get the publication by calling the IRS at (800) 829-3676 or you can download it from their Web site:

IRS WEB SITE
http://www.irs.gov

Preneed Arrangements   7

Death is a wake-up call because once someone close to us dies we are reminded of our own mortality. Many of us believe that death can be put off, but the inevitable is inevitable. Although we cannot change the fact of our death, we have the power to control the circumstances of our death by making preneed arrangements.

Preneed arrangements can be made so that you are buried in the manner you wish and where you wish. You can make arrangements that direct the kind of medical treatments you want to be given in the event you become seriously ill.

You can legally appoint someone to make your medical decisions in the event you are too ill to speak for yourself. If you let that person know how you feel about life support systems, autopsies and anatomical gifts then that person will be authorized to act on your behalf and will see to it that your wishes are carried out.

As this chapter will show, it is relatively simple and inexpensive to make such preneed arrangements.

MAKING BURIAL ARRANGEMENTS

When making burial arrangements for the decedent, you may decide to purchase one or more burial spaces nearby for yourself or other family members.

If the decedent was buried in the family plot, then this is the time to take inventory of the number of spaces left and who in the family expects to use those spaces.

If all of the spaces are taken and if you plan to be cremated, then as explained in Chapter 1, some cemeteries will allow an urn to be placed in an occupied family plot. You can call the cemetery and ask them to explain their policy as it relates to the burial of an urn in a currently occupied grave site or mausoleum.

If this is not an option, and the cemetery of your choice has a columbarium, you might consider purchasing a space at this time.

If you wish to have your cremains scattered, then you need to let your next of kin know where and how this is to be done.

VETERAN OR
VETERAN'S SPOUSE

If you are an honorably discharged veteran, you have the right to be buried in a Veterans National Cemetery. You cannot reserve a grave site in advance. If your Veteran spouse was buried in a Veterans National Cemetery then you have the right to be buried in that same grave site unless soil conditions require a separate grave site.

If you wish to be buried in a Veterans National Cemetery, then check on current availability (see page 14 for telephone numbers). Let your next of kin know your choice of cemetery.

To establish your eligibility your next of kin will need to provide the following information:

➤ the veteran's rank, serial, social security and VA claim numbers

➤ the branch of service; the date and place of entry into and separation from the service

The next of kin will also need to provide the VA with a copy of the veteran's official military discharge document bearing an official seal or a DD 214 form.

If you wish to be buried in a national cemetery, then make all of these items readily accessible to your family.

MAKING FUNERAL ARRANGEMENTS

If you are financially able, in addition to purchasing a burial space, consider purchasing a Preneed funeral plan. It will be easier on your family emotionally and financially if you make your own funeral arrangements. If you do not have sufficient cash on hand for the kind of funeral you desire, then many funeral directors offer an installment payment plan.

Once you decide on a plan, the funeral director will present you with a contract. The print may be small, but it is worth your effort to read it before signing. If the contract is written in "legalese" then either consult with your attorney before signing it or ask as many questions of the funeral director as is necessary to make the terms of the contract clear to you.

If you are not satisfied with the way a certain section of the contract is written then add an addendum to the contract that explains, in plain English, your understanding of that passage. If you are concerned about something that is not mentioned in the contract, then insist that the contract be amended to include that item.

In particular, check to see whether the contract answers the following questions.

How are your contract funds protected?

Michigan laws are designed to protect the purchaser of a Preneed Funeral Plan. Monies paid toward the contract price must be placed in escrow. The seller of a Preneed Funeral Contract may charge a commission of up to 10% of the contract price. The commission is not placed in escrow. The seller can serve as escrow agent, but not if the Preneed Plan is a guaranteed price, i.e. fixed price, contract. In those cases a financial institution (bank, credit union, trust company, etc.) must serve as escrow agent.

Michigan law requires that you be given written notice of the name and address of the escrow agent, and the amount on deposit. The law also requires that you be notified in the event the escrow agent or depository is changed. You may want to have these provisions included into your contract together with a promise that such notice will be sent to you within 30 days.

Michigan law also requires that you be given an annual accounting from the escrow agent stating the current balance, interest earned, and any service charge. The escrow agent is allowed to charge up to 1% of the account balance as a service fee (MCL 328.222, 328.224).

Your contract might contain a statement that you waive (give up) your right to an annual accounting. No doubt you will want such waiver deleted from the contract. You can do so by drawing a large line through the provision and then placing your initials next to the deletion. The seller will also need to initial the change.

Does the contract cover all costs?

The contract should contain an itemized list stating exactly what goods and services are included in the sales price. Ask the funeral director whether there will be any additional cost when you die. For example, if you have not purchased a burial space, then that cost needs to be factored in. If you made provision for a burial space, then you need to let the funeral director know where you have arranged to be buried. If you have not made such provision, then the funeral director can assist you in making burial arrangements.

Is the price guaranteed?

Some Preneed plans have a fixed price for the goods and services you chose. You are guaranteed that the goods and services will be provided upon your death, regardless of when you finally die. Sometimes the person who is selling the contract is not the same person who will provide the goods and services. If that is the case, then Michigan law requires that provider of the goods and services either sign your Preneed Contract, or your contract needs to refer to a written agreement between the seller of the contract and the provider of the goods and services (MCL 328.221). You need to verify who is going to actually provide the goods and services. If your contract refers to a contract between the seller and provider, you may want to read such an agreement to be sure that provider has agreed to honor your contract.

If the price for the goods and services that you have chosen under Preneed Contract is are not fixed, then the company can charge additional monies upon your death. In these days of an ever increasing life expectancy, it is important that such a contract clearly state how the price will be determined when the contract is finally put into effect.

Is the funeral firm reputable?

All these precautions don't do much good if you are not dealing with a reputable company. It is important to take the time to check up on whoever is selling you the contract. In Michigan, anyone who offers Preneed contracts to the public must be licensed to do so (MCL 328.216). You can check to see if the seller is licensed by calling the State Licensing Board at (519) 241-9252. You may also want to ask how long they have been in business and whether any complaints have been filed against them.

Can you cancel the contract?

Michigan law gives you the right to cancel your Prepaid Funeral Contract at any time. If you revoke the contract within 10 business days, then you have the right to receive all of you monies back. After that you will probably forfeit the monies you paid as a commission. To cancel, you will need to give the seller 30 days notice. The seller will notify the escrow agent to refund your money. If you paid a commission of more than 5%, then you are entitled to 100% of the monies paid. If you paid up to 5%, then you are entitled to 95% of the monies in escrow. If you have not paid any commission, then the seller is entitled to 10% of the monies in escrow (MCL 328.223, 328.225).

If you intend to pay for your Prepaid Funeral on an installment basis, then you need to know how much of the monies you pay will be returned to you in the event you default on payment.

THE IRREVOCABLE CONTRACT

People who are applying for, or receiving, Medicaid, Supplemental Security Income ("SSI") or other public assistance program have limits on the amount of assets that they may own. If someone purchases a Prepaid Funeral Plan, then the monies paid into the plan count as an asset because the purchaser of the plan can revoke the contract and get his money back. Understanding the problem, Michigan law allows the applicant to purchase a an irrevocable Prepaid Funeral plan provided it is a guaranteed price contract of not more than $2,000. The state will pay for an outside receptacle if it is required by the cemetery. Of course the family is free to add to the funeral plan after the person is deceased and purchase a more expensive plan (MCL 328.229).

Suppose you die in another state or country?

It is a good idea to have the contract spell out what provision will be made in the event that you move to another state or in the event you happen to die in another state or country. Many funeral firms are part of a national funeral service corporation with funeral firms located throughout the United States. You may be able to have the contract provide that there will be no additional charge if the contract is performed by one of the funeral firms owned by the parent company.

Can the plan be changed after your death?

It may happen that your heirs need to change the plan after your death because:

➤ your body is missing or cannot be recovered, or

➤ you were buried by another facility because your heirs were unaware of your Preneed contract, or

➤ you died in another country and were buried there.

Or perhaps your heirs decide on a plan different than the one you purchased. Funeral firms generally allow heirs to make changes to the plan you paid for such as:

➤ purchasing a more expensive plan and paying the difference

➤ changing to a lesser plan and receiving a refund.

Under Michigan law, your Personal Representative has the same right as you do to cancel the contract and receive the monies you paid, less the commissions (MCL 328.223).

You may wonder why anyone would think of changing the decedent's funeral plan, but consider that in today's market, it is not uncommon for a Preneed contract to cost several thousand dollars. A top end funeral complete with solid bronze casket can cost upwards of $40,000.

And there may be other motivations. Consider the case of Mona, a difficult woman with a personality that can only be described as "sour." Her husband deserted her after four years of marriage leaving her to raise their son, Lester, by herself. Once Lester was grown, Mona made it clear to him that she had done her job and now he was on his own. Lester could have used some help. He married and had three children. One of his children suffered with asthma and it was a constant struggle to keep up with the medical bills.

Mona believed in being good to herself. She did not intend to, nor did she, leave much money when she died. She knew that Lester would not be able to afford a "proper" burial for her, so she purchased a funeral plan and paid close to $18,000 for it. She was pleased when the funeral director told her that the monies would be kept safely in an escrow account until the time they were needed.

Lester was not familiar with Michigan law, so when Mona died he asked an attorney at the Legal Aid office to determine whether the Preneed contract was revocable.

It was.

You know the ending to this story.

If you are concerned that you get the exact type of funeral that you want, with no changes, then your attorney can suggest any number of ways to do so. The simplest way may be to purchase an irrevocable Preneed Funeral Plan and then give someone a Durable Power of Attorney to conduct the funeral in the manner you wish. See Chapter 10 for a discussion of the Durable Power of Attorney.

You may be thinking "Revocable, Irrevocable. All this contract stuff is giving me a headache. Why can't I just set aside some money and let my kids figure it out?"

The problem with that approach is the cost of your final days may leave you with little or no funds for your burial. To avoid the problem, you could purchase a life insurance policy to fund your funeral and burial, naming one or two trusted family members as the beneficiary of the policy. It is important that the person who is to receive the insurance funds clearly understands why he/she is named as beneficiary of the policy. It is equally important that the beneficiary agree to use the monies for the intended purpose.

It isn't so much that a family member is not trustworthy as it is that they may not understand what you intended, especially in those cases where other funds are available to pay for the funeral. Too often insurance funds are left to a child who then refuses to contribute to the cost of the funeral saying in effect "Dad wanted me to have this money — that's why he left it to me."

To avoid a misunderstanding, put it in writing. It need not be a formal contract. It could be something as simple as a letter to the insurance beneficiary, with copies to your next of kin. The next page contains a sample letter.

Dear Romita,

I purchased a $20,000 insurance policy today naming you as beneficiary of the policy. As we discussed this money is to be used to pay for the following:
- my funeral and grave site
- my headstone
- perpetual care for my grave
- airfare for each of my grandchildren
   to attend the funeral
- dinner for the family after the wake
- lunch for the family after the funeral

If there is any money left over, please accept it as my thanks for all the effort spent on my behalf.

Love,
 Dad

P.S. I am sending a copy of this letter to your brother so that he will know that all arrangements have been made.

Whether or not you arrange to pay for your burial or funeral, you need to let your next of kin know your feelings about the burial procedure. Let your family know whether you wish to be cremated or buried. If you wish to have a religious service, then let your family know the type of service and where it is to be held. Let the family know where you wish to be buried, or if you intend to be cremated, then where to place the ashes.

ANATOMICAL GIFTS

If you want to make an anatomical gift to take effect upon your death, you can make the gift as part of your Will; but it may be some time before your Will is located. The better route is to make the donation by a separate writing. Michigan statute 333.10104 contains a form that you can complete. You can download the statute from the Michigan statute Web site:

http://www.michiganlegislature.org/law

You can also complete an organ donor card when you apply for your Michigan driver's license or if you do not drive, then when you apply for your Official Michigan State Personal Identification Card (MCL 28.292).

If you are aged, and in poor health, the Transplantation Society of Michigan will probably not consider your body for transplantation of body parts, but you can still donate your body for education and research. If you wish to make such as donation, call or write to any local school of medicine. The school will forward a Dedication Form to you along with information on the subject. As discussed on page 6, there is no charge for local transportation to the school. But there may be a substantial cost should you die far from the school. If you make a gift, then give your family instructions about what to do in the event that you die far from home.

If you do not wish to make an anatomical gift, then let your family know how you feel.

AUTOPSIES
As discussed in Chapter 1, some autopsies are optional. If you have strong feelings about allowing an optional autopsy or not allowing the procedure, then let your family know how you feel.

Of course, there are problems with just telling someone how you feel about your burial arrangements, autopsies, and anatomical gifts:

THE PERSON DOES NOT CARRY OUT YOUR WISHES
Without written instructions, your next of kin will decide and then authorize the disposition of your remains. Whether they authorize an anatomical gift or an autopsy may depend more about how they feel about the procedure than what you wish.

Sometimes the person you tell may not understand what you said or perhaps they hear only what they want to hear. An example that comes to mind is the mother who complained that she felt like a burden to her children. She would often say "When I die, burn my body and throw my ashes out to sea." Her children paid no attention. No one asked, nor did they even think about, what she may have really wanted. When she died she was given a full funeral and buried in a local cemetery.

Even if you tell someone and trust that person to carry out your wishes, it could be that the person you confide in cannot carry out your instructions. For example, if you tell your spouse what arrangements to make, then he/she may become incapacitated or die before you do; or perhaps you both die simultaneously in a natural disaster or in a plane crash.

YOU TELL THE WRONG PERSON

You may tell someone who does not have authority to carry out your wishes. That was the case with James. Once his wife died, he moved to a retirement community where he lived for 15 years until his death.

James had two sons who lived in different states. Although he loved his sons, he had difficulty talking to either of them about serious matters. It was easier for him to talk with his friends in the retirement community. They often spoke about dying and how they felt about different burial arrangements. James would reminisce about his youth and growing up in a farming community in the plains state of Kansas. "I was happy and free. Out there you had room to breathe. It would be nice to be buried there — peaceful and spacious."

When he died, his friends told his sons about their father's desire to be buried in Kansas. They met the suggestion with scepticism and pragmatism:

"Dad didn't say anything like that to me."

"It would cost us double, if we had to arrange for burial in another state. I'm sure he didn't have that kind of expense in mind."

WHO WANTS TO TALK ABOUT IT?

For many people the main problem with telling someone what to do when you die is talking about your death. It may be an uncomfortable, if not unpleasant, subject for you to bring up, and for your family to discuss. If this is the case, then consider putting the information in writing and give the instructions to the person who will have the job of carrying out your wishes.

APPOINTING A PATIENT ADVOCATE

You can legally appoint someone to make your medical decisions in the event that you are too ill to do so yourself. The person you appoint is called a *Patient Advocate*, and the document appointing the advocate is called *Patient Advocate Designation*. There is no statutory form of the Patient Advocate Designation, but Michigan statute 700.5507 does contain specific regulations about the document and its application.

To be legally enforceable a Patient Advocate Designation must be in writing and signed by the *Patient* (the person making the designation) in the presence of two disinterested witnesses; i.e., the witness cannot be the person chosen to be Advocate, nor a beneficiary of the Patient's estate, nor the Patient's physician, nor any employee of the Patient's insurance provider, nor any employee of the Patient's health care facility. This means that the Patient needs to sign the Designation in advance of being placed in a hospital or nursing home, or else they will need to bring in two independent witnesses if they need to sign once admitted to a hospital or nursing home (MCL 700.5506).

You may be thinking "Why bother with a Patient Advocate? I probably will never need anyone to assist me. And even if I did, my family will tell the doctor what I want."

Those were George's thoughts exactly, even though his attorney advised him differently: "George, you are a man of substantial wealth and have made good provision for the care of your finances in the event of your incapacity, but you also need to make provision for someone to make your medical decisions in the event that you are too sick to make them yourself. This is easily done by signing a Patient Advocate Designation."

George said "My wife Loretta is a lovely lady, but she and my son from my first marriage are always at odds. If I choose one, the other would be hurt."

The attorney suggested "If you don't want to appoint a Patient Advocate, then at least let people know what kind of medical treatment you want in the event that you are too ill to speak for yourself. For example, do you want intravenous feeding in the event that you are so ill that there is no hope of recovery?"

"You mean sign a Living Will?"

"We do not have a statutory form of Living Will here in Michigan. Our current statute (MCL 700.5507) does allow you to include specific written instructions, as part of your Patient Advocate Designation, giving your Advocate authority to have treatment withheld or withdrawn in the event that you are mortally ill."

George said he would think about it. But he didn't.

The attorney's advice turned out to be prophetic. George suffered a stroke while driving a car. His injuries from the accident combined with the severity of the stroke made for a bleak prognosis. The doctors said George would die unless they put him on a ventilator and inserted a feeding tube. Even with life support systems, it was not expected that he would ever come out of the coma.

Loretta told the doctors "Let's try everything to keep him alive."

George's son did not see it that way. "Why torture him with needles and tubes? Let him pass on peacefully."

George never told anyone how he felt about artificial life support systems. He never signed a Patient Advocate Designation, so his doctors didn't know who George would have wanted to speak on his behalf. The doctors were caught in the middle, and rather than risk a law suit, they decided to bring the matter before a court and ask a judge to appoint a Guardian who would have authority to direct the treatment.

Loretta petitioned the court to be appointed as George's guardian. So did his son. The court battle over who was to be George's guardian was bitter (and expensive).

Before Loretta and George married they signed a prenuptial agreement. The agreement provided for each to give up all rights to inherit property from the other. Loretta had little money of her own. George's son accused Loretta of thinking of her own best interest and not of his father. If George were to die, Loretta would be on her own.

Loretta made the same accusation against her stepson. She said that the only thing the son was interested in was inheriting his father's fortune as quickly as possible.

The Judge determined that George had not been overly generous with his son. His son was married and raising his own family. Without any help from his father, he was struggling to support his family. The Judge also found that Loretta's life style would change significantly should George die.

Under Michigan law, the spouse has priority of appointment over the adult child (MCL 700.5313). However, in this case the Judge found neither spouse or child to be qualified to serve as George's Guardian. The Judge ruled that each of the parties had a conflict of interest and could be prejudiced by his/her own circumstances. He appointed a professional, independent, Guardian to make medical decisions for George.

The Guardian conferred with the doctors and determined that it was futile to continue life support systems.

George died.

Everyman's Estate Plan

The first six chapters of this book describe how to wind up the affairs of the decedent. As you read those chapters, you learned about the kinds of problems that can occur when settling the decedent's estate. It is relatively simple for you to set up an estate plan so that your family members are not burdened with similar problems. An *Estate Plan* is the arranging of one's finances to reduce (if not eliminate) Probate costs and estate taxes, and to ensure that your property is transferred quickly and at little cost.

If you think that only wealthy people need to prepare an estate plan, you are mistaken. Each year, heirs of relatively modest estates, spend thousands of dollars to settle an estate. A bit of planning could have eliminated most, if not all, of the expense and hassle suffered by those families.

The suggestions in this chapter are designed to assist the average person in preparing a practical and inexpensive estate plan, so we have named this chapter EVERYMAN'S ESTATE PLAN.

Once you create your own estate plan, you can be assured that your family will not be left with more problems than happy memories of you.

AVOIDING PROBATE

TRUE OR FALSE?

( )   If you have a Will, then there will need
      to be a Probate administration.

( )   If you don't have a Will, then Probate is necessary.

( )   Probate is necessary if the decedent owned
      anything worth more than $15,000.

If you answered false to all of the, then you are either a lawyer or you carefully read chapters 5 and 6.

For those who do not enjoy "Pop Quizzes," please forgive our reversion to educator (or maybe pedantic). The point we were attempting to make is that:

> Whether a Probate procedure is necessary has nothing to do with whether there is a Will, or even how much money is involved. The determining factor is how the property is titled (owned).

There are three ways to title property:

    ✧ jointly with another

    ✧ in trust for another

    ✧ in your name only.

In general, property held jointly or in trust for someone goes directly to the intended beneficiary without the need for Probate. There may need to be a Probate procedure if property is held in the decedent's name only.

In this chapter we explore the pros and cons of titling property in each of the three ways, beginning with holding property jointly with another.

OWNERSHIP OF BANK ACCOUNTS

You can arrange to have all of your bank accounts set up so that should you die, the money goes directly to a beneficiary. For example, suppose all you own is a bank account and you want whatever you have in this account to go to your son and daughter when you die. You might think that a simple solution is to put each child's name on the account, but first consider the problems associated with a joint account:

⊠ POTENTIAL LIABILITY

If you hold a bank account jointly with your adult child and that child is sued or gets a divorce then the child may need to disclose his ownership of the joint account. In such a case, you may find yourself spending money to prove that the account was established for convenience only and that all of the money in that account really belongs to you.

⊠ OVERREACHING

If you set up a joint account with your child so that the child has authority to withdraw funds from the account, then funds may be withdrawn without your authorization. If you open a joint account with two of your children, then after your death the first child to the bank may decide to withdraw all of the money and that will, at the very least, cause hard feelings between them.

⊠ THE MINOR CHILD

In Michigan, a minor can own a savings or checking account alone or jointly with another. A minor can lease a safe deposit box in his name only or jointly with another. But if you make a minor the joint owner of your account, would you want the child to be able to remove money from your account? Would you want the minor to be able to go to the bank and withdraw everything in your safe deposit box?

Because of these inherent problems, you might want to hold the funds so that your beneficiary does not gain access to the monies until and unless you die. There are three ways to do so: the "in trust for" account, the "pay on death" account and "transfer on death" account.

You can direct a financial institution to hold your account *in trust for* ("ITF") a beneficiary that you name. During your lifetime you have complete control over the account. You can add to it or close it out entirely without permission from or notice to your beneficiary. The beneficiary does not have access to the account until and unless you die. Should you die while the account is operational, the bank will turn over the funds to the beneficiary.

In Michigan, the *Pay On Death* ("POD") or a *Transfer On Death* ("TOD) account are more commonly used to maintain complete control of the property during the account owner's lifetime, and then have it transferred to a beneficiary after death without the need for Probate. In some states the POD designation is reserved for bank accounts or Certificates of Deposit, and the TOD designation is reserved for stocks, bonds, or securities accounts. In Michigan, no distinction is made. Both of these are referred to as a registration in *Beneficiary Form* (MCL 700.6301, 700.6305).

BENEFICIARY DIES FIRST
Should the beneficiary of the account die before the owner of the account, then unless the owner of the account has made some other provision with the financial institution, the account goes to the estate of the owner of the account (MCL 700.6307). The next page contains different ways to make provision for an alternate beneficiary.

You can open a beneficiary account with instructions to give the money to your child when you die, and if the child dies before you, then to your grandchildren in equal shares, per stirpes. For example:

Eldon Connors POD Betty Connors LDPS

which is short-hand for:

"ELDON CONNORS is the owner of the account. On his death, pay all of the account funds to BETTY CONNORS, but if she dies first, then give it to her lineal descendants in equal shares, per stirpes" (MCL 700.6310).

There may be times when you wish to hold a Beneficiary Account jointly (say with your spouse) and have your children inherit the account when you both die. For example, the account could be titled:

ELDON CONNORS and LORRAINE CONNORS, JT TEN
TOD SUSAN CONNORS AND FRED CONNORS, JT TEN

⇨ The children (Susan and Fred) have no right to the account during the lifetime of their parents.

⇨ If either Eldon or Lorraine dies, then the surviving party owns the account, and is free to close the account or change the beneficiary of the account.

⇨ Once Eldon and Lorraine are deceased, their children share the money in the account equally.

⇨ Susan and Fred are joint beneficiaries of the account. If one of the children dies before the parent dies, then the remaining child gets all of the money in the account (MCL 700.6302, 700.6304, 700.6306).

If your Estate consists only of bank accounts and/or securities, and you want all of your property to go to one or two beneficiaries without the need for Probate, but with maximum control and protection of your funds during your lifetime, then holding your property in any of these beneficiary forms:

"In Trust For"
"Pay-On-Death"
"Transfer-On-Death"

should accomplish your goal.

 **FINANCIAL INSTITUTIONS ARE REGULATED DIFFERENTLY**

In Michigan, there are separate statutory codes for different kinds of financial institutions doing business within the state. Banks are subject to the Banking Code of 1999 (MCL 487.11101, et seq.). Savings Banks are subject to the Savings Bank Act (MCL 487.3101, et seq.); while Savings and Loan Associations are regulated by the Savings and Loan Act of 1980 (MCL 491.102, et seq.) Credit Unions are regulated by a separate chapter of the Compiled Laws (MCL 490.1, et seq.). The Codes quoted on the previous page were regulations from the Estates and Protected Individuals Code Act of 1998. That Code deals with the manner in which property is transferred upon the death of the owner of an account in Beneficiary form. When setting up an account, you need to read your agreement with the financial institution to be sure that your property will be transferred according to your wishes.

GIFT TO MINOR

At the beginning of this chapter, we identified two problems with a joint account: potential liability if the joint owner is sued and overreaching by the joint owner. If you wish to make a gift to a minor child, then that presents still another problem. The ITF, POD and TOD account avoid the problems of potential liability and overreaching, but if the beneficiary of such account is a minor, there is the problem of the child having access to a large sum of money. A company in possession of the funds may give amounts up to $10,000 to a trust company or to an adult member of the child's family. The company will not transfer funds over $10,000 without seeking permission from the Probate Court. The Court may decide to appoint a Conservator to care for the property until the child reaches 18.

This presents a dilemma. If the amount given is no greater than $10,000, and the company decides to give the money to the parent, all of the funds may be spent to care for the child. The child may never even know of your gift. You may think it best that the child inherits more than $10,000; this way a Court will see to it that the monies are held safely till the child reaches 18. But that only presents a new set problem. It takes time, effort and money to set up a conservatorship. If you leave the child a significant amount of money, then the Conservator has the right to be paid to manage those funds. It could happen that the cost of the conservatorship significantly reduces the amount of money inherited by the child. There are ways to avoid the problem of having a Conservator appointed to care for property inherited by a child, and yet ensuring that the monies are protected. We will discuss those methods, in detail, in the next chapter.

THE GIFT OF REAL PROPERTY

As explained in Chapter 5, if you own real property together with another, then who will own the property upon your death depends on how the Grantee is identified on the face of the deed. If you compare the Grantee clause of the deed to the examples on pages 101 through 104 you can determine who will inherit that property should you die. If you are not satisfied with the way the property will be inherited, then you need to consult with an attorney to change the deed so that it will conform to your wishes.

If you own the property in your name only, then once you die, there will need to be a Probate procedure to determine the proper beneficiary of that parcel of land. If your main objective is to avoid Probate, then you can have an attorney change the deed so that once you die, the property descends to your beneficiary without the need for Probate. As with bank and securities accounts there are different ways to do so, each with its own advantages and disadvantages.

JOINT OWNERSHIP
You can have your deed changed so that you and your intended beneficiary are joint owners with rights of survivorship. If you do so then should either of you die, the other will own the property 100%. This keeps the property out of Probate but you will not be able to sell that property during your lifetime without the beneficiary's permission. And if the beneficiary gives permission and the property is sold during your lifetime, the beneficiary will have the legal right to half of the proceeds of the sale.

CAUTION   GIFT OF HOMESTEAD

Some people think it a good idea to avoid Probate by transferring their homestead to their children, and just continue to live there. But this just creates a new set of problems:

⊠ RISK OF LOSS

If you transfer your homestead to a beneficiary it could be lost if the beneficiary runs into serious financial difficulties or gets sued. This is especially a risk if your child is a professional (doctor, nurse, accountant, financial planner, attorney, etc.). If your child is found to be personally liable for damages, then the house could be sold to satisfy the judgment.

If your child is (or gets) married, then this complicates matters even more so. If the child is divorced, the property could well be included as part of the settlement agreement. This may be to your child's detriment because the child may need to share the value of the property with his/her ex-spouse. If you do not transfer the property, then it cannot become part of the marital equation.

⊠ LOSS OF HOMESTEAD CREDITOR PROTECTION

Up to $3,500 of the value of your homestead is protected from creditors during your lifetime. Should a creditor (not a mortgagee) force the sale of your property, then at least you get to keep $3,500. The more important creditor protection is that for your spouse and minor child (see Page 89). If you transfer the property, you lose this protection for yourself and for your family (MCL 600.6023)

⊠   POSSIBLE LOSS OF GOVERNMENT BENEFITS

If you transfer property, then depending upon the value of the transfer, you could be disqualified from receiving Medicaid or Supplemental Security Income ("SSI") benefits for up to 3 years from the date of transfer. The federal and state rules that determine the period of ineligibility are complex. If nursing care could be a problem, then it is best to consult with an Elder Law attorney to prepare a Medicaid Estate Plan.

TAX CONCERNS FOR REAL PROPERTY TRANSFERS

Before you make a real estate transfer be it joint interest, life estate or outright gift, you need to consider the tax consequences of the transfer:

⊠   POSSIBLE GIFT TAX

If the value of the transfer is worth more than $10,000 you need to file a gift tax return. For most of us, this is not a problem because no gift tax need be paid unless the value of the property (plus the value of all gifts in excess of $10,000 per person, per year, that you gave over your lifetime) exceeds $1,000,000 (see Page 38).

If your estate is in that tax bracket, then you need to be aware that you are "using up" your tax credit.

⊠ LOSS OF HOMESTEAD TAX EXEMPTION

Each home owner in Michigan is entitled to a homestead tax exemption for property that they occupy as their principal residence. In addition there are special tax exemptions for the elderly or indigent or disabled and for veterans or their unremarried widows (MCL 211.7b, 211.7cc, 211.7d, 211.7dd) If you put the deed in the beneficiary's name and that property is your homestead, then you will lose your homestead tax exemption. It could cost more money in taxes to continue to live in your own home.

It may be possible to keep your homestead tax exemption by transferring the property to a beneficiary and keeping a life estate for yourself or holding the property jointly with the beneficiary. But, as explained, you will not be able to sell the property during your lifetime without the permission of all of the people you named as Grantee on the deed; and if you sell the property each Grantee is entitled to some portion of the proceeds of the sale.

If you decide to transfer your homestead to a beneficiary, before doing so, call the Michigan Department of Treasury (800) 487-7000 and ask them if there will be any tax consequence as a result of the transfer; and also what documents need to be filed once the transfer is made.

⊠ POSSIBLE CAPITAL GAINS TAX

There is no discussion in Congress to do away with the Capital Gains Tax. If you gift the property to the child, when he sells the property he will be subject to a Capital Gains Tax on the increase in value from the price you paid to the selling price at the time of the sale. If you do not make the gift during your lifetime, the child will inherit the property with a step-up in basis, i.e., he will inherit the property at its market value as of the date of death. Under today's tax structure and continuing until 2009, that step-up in basis is unlimited. Your child can immediately sell inherited property and pay no Capital Gains Tax, regardless of how large the step-up in basis. In 2010, there will be a limit on amount that can be inherited free of the Capital Gains Tax (see Page 37). Under the current law, the limit for a child is scheduled to be 1.3 million dollars, so for most of us, the limit in the step-up in basis is not a concern.

Some of the problems associated with an outright gift, may be avoided by transferring the property to your child while keeping a Life Estate for yourself. But, as with joint ownership, you will not be able to sell or transfer the property during your lifetime unless your child agrees to the transfer. And as with joint ownership, should you sell the property your child is entitled to some part of the proceeds of the sale.

Before making any real property transfer, it is important to consult with your accountant, and/or attorney, and/or certified financial planner, to examine all aspects related to the transfer.

OUT OF STATE PROPERTY

Each state is in charge of the way property located in that state is transferred. If you own property in another state (or country) then you need to consult with an attorney in that state (or country) to determine how that property will be transferred to your beneficiaries once you die. In Michigan, a deed held as Joint Tenants means that there are rights of survivorship, i.e., if one Joint Tenant dies, the remaining Joint Tenant(s) own the property without the need for Probate. But other states may require that the deed state that there are **rights of survivorship**. In such states, holding property as Joint Tenants is the same as holding property as Tenants-In-Common, and a Probate procedure will be necessary in order to transfer the property to the proper beneficiary.

It is important to determine whether a Probate procedure will be necessary to transfer property that you own in another state. If so, then it may take two Probate procedures to settle your estate. One in Michigan and another in the state where the property is located.

Still another problem is the matter of taxes. Some states have an inheritance or transfer tax. Estate taxes may be due in the state where the property is located as well as in Michigan. It may be necessary to file a tax return in two states. In addition to increased taxes, this can double the cost of the accounting fees.

You may wish to consult with an attorney for suggestions about how to set up your Estate Plan to avoid such problems.

A TRUST MAY BE THE SOLUTION (OR NOT)

A full Probate procedure may be necessary if you hold personal property in your name only that is worth more than $15,000, or if you hold real property as a Tenant-In-Common or in your name only. We explored different ways to re-title property to avoid Probate, but these methods may have trade-offs that are unacceptable to you. One way to avoid many of these potential problems is to set up a ***Revocable Living Trust*** (also known as an ***Inter Vivos Trust***).

A Revocable Living Trust is designed to care for your property during your lifetime and then to distribute your property once you die without the need for Probate. You may have been encouraged to set up such a Trust by your financial planner, or attorney, or accountant. Even people of modest means are being encouraged to use a Trust as the basis of their Estate Plan. But Trusts also have their pros and cons. Before getting into that, let's first discuss what a Trust is and how it works:

SETTING UP A TRUST

To create a Trust, an attorney prepares the Trust document in accordance with the client's needs and desires. The person who signs the document is called the ***Trustor*** or ***Settlor.*** If the ***Trustor*** also funds the Trust, then he is also referred to as the ***Grantor.*** We will refer to the Revocable Living Trust as the "Living Trust" or just the "Trust" and the person setting up the Trust as the "Grantor." The Trust document identifies who is to be the Trustee (manager) of property placed in the Trust. Usually the Grantor appoints himself as Trustee so that he is in total control of property that he places into the Trust. The Trust document also names a Successor Trustee who will take over the management of the Trust property should the Trustee resign, or become disabled or die.

Once the Trust document is properly signed, the Grantor transfers property into the Trust. The Grantor does this by changing the name on the account from his individual name to his name as Trustee. For example, if Elaine Richards sets up a Trust naming herself as Trustee, and she wishes to place her bank account into the Trust then all she need do is instruct the bank to change the name on the account from ELAINE RICHARDS to:

ELAINE RICHARDS, TRUSTEE of the ELAINE RICHARDS REVOCABLE TRUST AGREEMENT DATED JULY 12, 2001.

When the change is made, all the money in the account becomes Trust property. Elaine (wearing her Trustee hat) has total control of the account, taking money out, and putting money in, as she sees fit. Similarly, if she wants to put real property into the Trust all she need do is have her attorney prepare a new deed with the Grantee identified as ELAINE RICHARDS, TRUSTEE (see page 107 for an example of real property placed into a Trust).

The Trust document states how the Trust property is to be managed during Elaine's lifetime. Should Elaine become disabled the Trust will provide for her Successor Trustee to take over and manage the Trust funds. Because the Trust is revocable, if she wishes, Elaine can terminate the Trust at any time and have all the Trust property returned and placed back into her own individual name. If she does not revoke her Trust during her lifetime, then once she dies the Trust becomes irrevocable, and her Successor Trustee must follow the terms of the Trust Agreement as written. If the Trust says to give the Trust property to certain beneficiaries, then the Successor Trustee will do so; and in most cases without any Probate procedure. If the Trust directs the Successor Trustee to continue to hold property in Trust and use the money to take care of a member of Elaine's family, then the Successor Trustee will do so.

THE GOOD PART
Setting up a Trust has many good features.

☆☆ AVOID PROBATE
In Michigan, Probate can be time consuming and very expensive. Both the Personal Representative and his attorney are entitled to payment for their services. These fees can be significant. It may be necessary to hire accountants and appraisers, as well. If you have property in two states, then two Probate procedures may be necessary (one in each state) and that could have the effect of doubling the cost of Probate. If the Trust is properly drafted and your property placed into the Trust, you should be able to avoid Probate altogether.

☆ PRIVACY
Your Living Trust is a private document. No one but your Successor Trustee and your beneficiaries need ever read it. If you leave a Will and the Will needs to be probated, it will be filed with the court where it becomes a public document (MCL 700.2515). Anyone can go to the courthouse, read your Will and see who you did (or did not) provide for in your Will. It is not much of a stretch to predict that in the future, all Probate Court records (Wills, inventories, creditor's claims) will be available on the Internet!

☆ AVOID APPOINTMENT OF A CONSERVATOR
If you become disabled or too aged to handle your finances, then you do not need to worry about who takes care of your finances. The person you appointed as Successor Trustee will take over the care of the Trust property if you are unable to do so. If you do not have a Trust and you become incapacitated, a court may need to appoint a Conservator to care for your property. The cost to establish and maintain the Conservatorship is charged to you. And that can be very expensive.

☆ CARE FOR A CHILD OR FAMILY MEMBER:

You can make provision in your Trust to care for a child or family member after you die. If your family member is immature or a born spender, you can set up a Spendthrift Trust to protect him/her from squandering the inheritance. You can direct your Successor Trustee to use Trust funds to pay for the family member's health care, education or living expenses, and nothing more.

☆ TAX SAVINGS

Many people think that the Estate Tax will be phased out so that by 2010, no Estate Taxes will be due regardless of the size of an estate. That's true for 2010, but the current law covers only the period from 2001 to 2010. The Estate Tax is scheduled to be reinstated on January 1, 2011 and estates worth more than $1,000,000 will once again be subject to a sizeable Estate Tax. A couple with an estate in excess of a million dollars can reduce the risk of an Estate Tax by setting up his and her Trusts, so that each person can take advantage of his own Exemption Value (see Page 36). For example, if a couple own 2 million dollars, they can separate their funds into two Trusts each valued at one million dollars. Each Trust can be set up so that should one partner die, the surviving spouse can use the income from the deceased partner's Trust for living expenses. In this way, their standard of living need not be reduced by separating their funds into two Trusts. Once both partners are deceased, the beneficiaries of their respective Trusts will inherit the funds, hopefully with no Estate Tax due.

If the couple do not set up his/her Trusts and continue to hold their property jointly, then the last to die will own the two million dollars with only one tax Exemption available.

THE PROBLEMS

With all these perks, you may be ready to call your attorney to make an appointment to set up a Trust, but before doing so there are a few things you need to consider:

⊠ COMPLEXITY

A Trust is a fairly complex document, often 20 pages long. It needs to be that long because you are establishing a vehicle for taking care of your property during your lifetime, as well as after your death. The Trust usually is written in "legalese," so it may take you considerable time and effort to understand it. It is important to have your Trust document prepared by an attorney who has the patience to work with you until you fully understand each paragraph of the document and are satisfied that this is what you want.

⊠ PROBATE MIGHT STILL BE NECESSARY

The Trust only works for those items that you place in the Trust. If you have property that is held jointly with another, when you die, that property will go to the joint owner and not to the Trust. If you purchase a security in your name only, and forget to put it in your Trust, a Probate procedure may be necessary to determine who should inherit that security. The attorney who prepares the Trust usually creates a safety net for such a situation by having you sign a "Pour Over Will" at the same time you sign your Trust. The purpose of the Will is to "pour" any asset titled in your name only, into the Trust; specifically, the Will directs your Personal Representative, to put any asset held in your name only, into your Trust. This ensures that all of your property will go to the beneficiaries named in your Trust. But the downside, is that a Probate procedure may be necessary to get the asset into the Trust. This defeats a major goal of the Trust, namely to avoid Probate.

⊠ NO CREDITOR PROTECTION

Because property held in a Revocable Living Trust is freely accessible to the Grantor, it is likewise accessible to his creditors both before and after the Grantor's death. If the Grantor dies owing money, then his creditors can require that a Personal Representative be appointed to locate funds to pay those debts. The Personal Representative can require that your Trust funds be used to pay for those debts.

Even if no Personal Representative is appointed, the Trustee has a legal duty to use Trust funds to pay all debts associated with the Grantor's death of the Grantor, including the funeral and burial expenses, and the Homestead, Family and Exempt Property Allowances (MCL 700.7501, 700.7502)).

⊠ TRUST SUBJECT TO DOWER RIGHTS

A woman has Dower rights in all real property owned by her spouse (see page 105). If you are a married man at the time you set up your Trust, then you need your wife's permission to transfer real property into the Trust. If your wife does not release her Dower rights in property placed into the Trust, then regardless of what your Trust document says, she can assert those rights should you die before she does. If you are a married woman and you agree to the transfer of real property into your husband's Trust either by signing the deed transferring the property into the Trust, then you are giving up all of your Dower rights in that property (MCL 558.13).

☒   TAXES MAY STILL BE A PROBLEM:

While the Grantor is operating the Trust as Trustee, all of the property held in a Revocable Living Trust is taxed as if the Grantor were holding that property in his/her own name. If the value of the Trust property exceeds the Estate and Gift Tax Exemption Value, then unless the Grantor takes another, more advanced, Estate Planning strategy, taxes will be due and owing once the Grantor dies.

☒ ☆   THE TRUST IS LEGALLY ENFORCEABLE

Any beneficiary of the Trust can require your Successor Trustee to register the Trust with the Probate court in the county as stated in the Trust document (MCL 700.7104). If no county is stated, then in the county where the Trust is being administered. The Probate court can hear any dispute relating to the Trust and can order that the Trustee to live up to the terms of the Trust agreement (MCL 700.7101, 700.7103, 700.7201)

We gave this section a cross and a star, because the right to have a Trust enforced by the Probate court is a double edged sword. It is great to have a court ensure that the Trust is administered as you wish, but the cost of a court battle could be greater than using Probate to distribute your estate. Worse yet, your beneficiaries are at a disadvantage because the Trustee can charge the legal expenses to your Trust, while the beneficiaries must pay for their legal fees out of their own pocket.

Even if the beneficiaries win the argument, the Trustee's legal fees are paid from the Trust, so there is just that much less for the beneficiaries to inherit.

⊠ COST

Because of the thoroughness of the document and the fact that it is custom designed for you, a Trust will cost much more to draft than a simple Will. In addition to the initial cost of the Trust, it can be expensive to maintain the Trust should you become disabled or die. Your Successor Trustee has the right to charge for his duties as Trustee, as well as to charge for any specialized services performed.

If you choose an attorney to be Successor Trustee, the attorney has the right to charge to manage the Trust, and also charge for any legal work he performs. A financial institution can charge to serve as Successor Trustee, and also charge to manage the Trust portfolio. A Successor Trustee who is a family member may not want to take any compensation.

Regardless of whether you choose a professional or a family member to be Successor Trustee, you need to come to an agreement with the Successor Trustee as to their compensation. The fee agreement can be included in the Trust document or you can have a separate fee agreement. If you do not make a written provision for fees, there could be a dispute between your beneficiaries and your Successor Trustee. If the dispute cannot be resolved between the parties, the Probate Court will hear evidence as to the going rate for Trustees of similar Trusts, and then order that amount be paid from the Trust. (MCL 700.7205).

MAYBE PROBATE ISN'T ALL THAT BAD

Although all of the methods discussed in this Chapter can be used to transfer property without the need for Probate, it may be each method has a downside that is objectionable to you. Maybe you don't have enough money to warrant the cost of setting up the Trust at this time. Holding property jointly with another may raise issues of security and independence. Holding property so that it goes directly to a few beneficiaries in a POD, TOD, or ITF account, may not be as flexible as you wish. This is especially the case if you wish to give gifts to several charities or to minor children instead of just one or two beneficiaries. For example, if you hold all your property so that it goes to your son without the need for Probate, and you ask him to use some of the money for your grandchild's education, it may be that your grandchild gets none of the money because your son is sued or falls upon hard times. If you keep your property in your name only and leave a Will giving a certain amount of money for your grandchild, then the child will know exactly how much money you left and the purpose of that gift.

After taking into account all the pros and cons of avoiding Probate, you may well opt for a Will and a Probate procedure. If you make such a decision, it is important to keep in mind that Estate Planning is not an "all or nothing" choice. You can arrange your estate so that certain items pass automatically to your intended beneficiary, and other items can be left in your name only, to be distributed as part of a Probate procedure. By arranging your finances in this manner, you can reduce the value of your Probate estate, and that in turn should reduce the cost of Probate.

YOUR WILL — YOUR WAY

Many people decide that the Will is the best route to go but do not act upon it, thinking it unnecessary to prepare a Will until they are very old and about to die. But according to reports published by the National Center for Health Statistics (a division of the U.S. Department of Health and Human Services) 2 of every 10 people who die in any given year are under the age of 60. Twenty percent may seem like a small number until it hits close to home as it did with one young couple. The couple was having difficulty conceiving a child. They went from doctor to doctor until they met someone just beginning his practice. With his knowledge of the latest advances in medicine, he was able to help them. The birth of their child was a moment of joy and gratitude. The couple asked a nurse to take a picture of them all together — the proud parents, the newborn child and the doctor who made it all possible. Happiness radiated from the picture, but within 6 months, one of them would be dead.

You might think it was the child. An infant's life is so fragile. SIDS and all manner of childhood diseases can threaten a little one. But no, he grew up a healthy young man.

If you looked at the picture, you might guess the husband. Overweight and stressed out; his ruddy complexion suggested high blood pressure. He looked like a typical heart-attack-prone type A personality.
No, he was fine and went on to enjoy raising his son.

Probably the wife. She had such a difficult time with the pregnancy and the delivery was especially hard. Perhaps it was all too much for her.
No, she recovered and later had two more children.

It was the doctor who was killed in a three-way collision.

Though we all agree, that one never knows, still people put off making a Will figuring that if they die before getting around to it, Michigan law will take over and their property will be distributed in the manner that they would have wanted anyway. The problem with that logic is the complexity of the Michigan's Laws of Intestate Succession. If you are survived by a spouse, child, parent or sibling, then it isn't too difficult to figure out who will inherit your property. But if none of these survive you, the ultimate beneficiary of your property may not be the person you would have chosen, had you taken the time to do so.

Others think that it is not necessary to have a Will because they have arranged their finances so that all of their property will be inherited without the need for Probate. But money could come into your estate after your death. This could happen in any number of ways from winning the lottery and dying (of happiness no doubt) to receiving insurance funds after your death. For example, if you die in a house fire or flood the insurance company may need to pay for damage done to your property. In such case, a Personal Representative will need to be appointed and the monies distributed according to Michigan law.

If you die without a Will, the Personal Representative may not be the person you would have chosen. The monies may be distributed differently than you would have wished.

And there are other important reasons to make a Will:

CHOOSE YOUR PERSONAL REPRESENTATIVE

An important reason to make a Will is so that you can choose your Personal Representative. You can even set the amount of money he is to receive in your Will.

 ### THE PERSONAL REPRESENTATIVE CAN SEEK MORE MONEY

Your Personal Representative may find the job of settling your estate to be more work than he anticipated. He may decide to ask the Probate court to allow a greater fee than specified in the Will. The Court may think that the amount stated in the Will was the amount you wanted to spend, but not necessarily the amount agreed to by your Personal Representative. To avoid the problem, you can have your attorney draft a binding agreement with your Personal Representative and attach it to your Will. By signing the Agreement, your Personal Representative is promising to accept the fee as provided in the Will.

Having a separate fee agreement will not prevent your Personal Representative from asking the Court for more money, but with such an agreement, it will be harder to get the Court to agree to the increase (MCL 700.3719).

▤ MAKE GIFTS OF YOUR PERSONAL PROPERTY

Another benefit to making a Will is that you can make provision for who will get your personal property, including your car. If you make a gift of your car in your Will, then it will be relatively simple for your car to be transferred to the beneficiary. If you do not make a specific gift of your car, then it becomes part of your Probate Estate. Your Personal Representative will decide what to do with the car. He can sell it and include the proceeds of the sale in the estate funds to be distributed to your residuary beneficiaries; or he can give the car to one of the beneficiary of your estate as part of that beneficiary's share of the estate.

SMALL GIFTS MATTER

Many who have lost someone close to them report that the distribution of the personal property caused the greatest conflict. If there is no need for a Probate procedure and the decedent died without a Will, then the next of kin need to decide, among themselves, how personal property is to be distributed. Without guidance from the decedent and no Personal Representative with authority to make decisions, there could be much disagreement and hard feelings, as was the case in the example given on page 129.

If you make a Will, you can include the list in your Will and your Personal Representative will distribute your personal property according to your directions. Even if you do not have a Will you can give away your personal property just by making out a list of your possessions, indicating who is receive each item, and then signing the statement (See page 128). It is a good idea to get input from the family when composing your list. You might ask each member of your family to give you a list entitled "THINGS I WOULD LIKE TO HAVE," and then consider all of the lists when you make your decision.

▤ MAKE ADJUSTMENT FOR PRIOR GIFTS

You can make adjustments for gifts or loans given during your lifetime. For example, if you have loaned money to a family member and do not expect to be repaid, then you can deduct the loan from that person's inheritance. Of course, it may be that you are not concerned with inequities. That was the case of an aged woman with three children, Paul, Rita and Frank her youngest. Frank always seemed to need some assist from his mother. She often "lent" him money that he never repaid. Her other children were responsible and independent. Paul was married and had children of his own. He decided to purchase a house but was having trouble accumulating the down payment. His mother agreed to lend him the money. Paul and his wife offered to give his mother a mortgage on the property. The mother said a simple promissory note from Paul was sufficient, and she would have her attorney draft the note.

The attorney drafted the note but was concerned about the inequity: "You never made a Will. Were you to die, then each of your children will get the same amount of money. Unless Frank gives you a promissory note, all of the money you gave to him will not count towards his inheritance; but the balance owed on the promissory note will be subtracted from Paul's inheritance. And there is a law here in Michigan, that if one of your heirs dies before you do and his children inherit his share, then the debt will not be subtracted from the money they inherit (MCL 700.2110). It could happen that Paul dies before you do, then the money you gave to Paul and to Frank will not be included into your estate. Your daughter will, in effect, receive much less than did her brothers."

"It's O.K." replied the woman "I love all my children equally . . . some a little more equal than others."

Either parent has the right to name someone in their Will to be Guardian of their child in the event that the parent dies before the child is grown, and the other parent is unable to care for the child. It would be nice if both parents name the same person in their respective Wills to be Guardian, but the reality is that parents often disagree about who is best qualified to raise the child. If they name different people to serve as Guardian, then the Will of the last to die controls. If each parent nominates a different Guardian, and they die simultaneously, then the Judge will decide who is best suited for the job (MCL 700.5202).

Of course, of one parent dies and the other parent is able to care for the minor, no Guardian will be appointed. The surviving parent retains parental rights, regardless of who the deceased parent named to serve as Guardian.

D.I.Y.

No matter what your finances, you can afford to make a Will. If your funds are limited, you can always "do it yourself" by going to a law library and copying the Michigan statutory Will (MCL 700.2519). If you are connected to the Web, you can download the form from the Michigan Legislative Web site:

MICHIGAN STATUTE WEB SITE
http://www.michiganlegislature.org/law

The statutory form is easy to read and to complete. The important thing is that you do not sign your Will until you are in the presence of two people who can sign as witnesses. It is preferable that neither of the witnesses stand to inherit anything under your Will, but just the fact that a witness may be a beneficiary will not invalidate your Will or your gift to that witness (MCL 700.2505).

If you want to really do a professional job, then you can "self-prove" your Will. This means that you add a section to your Will verifying that you signed the Will voluntarily and that your two witnesses verify that you were over 18 of sound mind when you did so. There is a statutory form of the Self-Proof (MCL 700.2504). You can copy or download the statutory Self-Proof form at the same time you copy the statutory Will.

The Self-Proof section of the Will must be signed by a Notary Public, verifying that you and the witnesses signed the document. Once the Will is properly Self-Proved, it can be admitted into Probate without the need for the Judge to call in your witnesses to testify that when you signed the Will you were of sound mind and did so of your own free will.

STORING THE WILL

Once you sign your Will, you may wonder where to store it. If an attorney prepared the Will he may suggest that he place it in his vault for safekeeping. By doing so, he ensures that your heirs will need to contact him as soon as you die. This does not mean that they are required to employ him should a Probate procedure be necessary. It only means that he will have an opportunity for future employment. In exchange, he gives you a good value. Your Will is kept safely in his vault, and at sole cost to him. Should anything happen to that Will, then it is his responsibility to make good the loss. Before allowing your attorney to store the Will, you should get a receipt and something in writing that says:

⇨ The attorney accepts full responsibility for storage of the Will. Should it be lost or damaged, he will replace the document at no cost to you; and if you are deceased, he will, at no cost to your heirs, present sufficient evidence to the Court to accept a valid copy of the Will into Probate.

⇨ There will be no charge to you, or your heirs, for the storage and retrieval of the document.

With all of this cost and liability, many attorneys will agree only to store a copy of your Will. In such case, consider storing your Will with the Clerk of the Circuit Court in the county of your residence. You are free to retrieve the Will from the Clerk in the event that you move or decide to change your Will.

Regardless of where you choose to store your Will, let your Personal Representative know that you have a Will and how to retrieve it in the event of your death.

THE SAFE DEPOSIT BOX

Once you have a Will or Trust, you may decide to rent a safe deposit box to store the document and perhaps other valuable documents or property. As explained on page 75, if you hold a safe deposit box in your name only, then should you die, a Personal Representative will need to be appointed in order to get possession of the contents of the box. If you have arranged your finances to avoid Probate, then it is self defeating to have entry to a safe deposit box trigger a Probate procedure. To avoid the problem you can:

LEASE THE BOX AS TRUSTEE

One of the benefits of having a Living Trust, is that you can lease the safe deposit box in your name as Trustee. When you lease the safe deposit box you can direct the Lessor (usually a bank) that they are to allow your Successor Trustee free access to the safe deposit box in the event of your incapacity or death.

APPOINT AN AGENT

You can appoint someone to be your Agent with authority to enter the safe deposit box. You can appoint the Agent when you contract with the Lessor to rent the box; or you can have your attorney draft a Power of Attorney giving someone authority to conduct your business and to have access to your safe deposit box. Your Agent will be able to enter the box up until the time the Lessor is notified of your death.

LEASE THE BOX JOINTLY WITH ANOTHER

If you are married and hold the box jointly with your spouse, then your spouse has free access to the box in the event of your death. If you are single, and do not have a Living Trust, then consider leasing the box jointly with a Trusted family member. Of course, if privacy and security are important to you, then that may offset any issue of convenience for your heirs.

CHOOSING THE RIGHT ESTATE PLAN

Joint Ownership?
An "in trust for" account?
A POD Account?
A TOD Security?
A Trust?
A Will?
An Insurance Policy???

This chapter offers so many options that the reader may be more confused than when he was blissfully unenlightened.

As with most things in life, you may find there are no ultimate solutions, just alternatives. The right choice for you is the one that best accomplishes your goal. This being the case, you first need to determine what you want to accomplish with the money that you leave. Think about what will happen to your property if you were to die suddenly, without making any plan different from the one you now have.

Who will get your property?
Will there be any estate tax?
Will Probate be necessary?

If the answers to these questions are not what you wish, then you need to work to retitle your property to accomplish your goals. For those with significant assets, — especially those with estates large enough to pay estate taxes, a trip to an experienced Estate Planning attorney may be well worth the consultation fee.

Continuing To Care 9

There are any number of reasons that people give for wanting to continue on with their life. For the lucky ones, their main reason for living is that they are having a great time and don't want it to end. For many, it is a more a sense of responsibility. During child rearing years the concern of the parent is what will happen to the child should the parent suddenly die. Once a child is grown, the roles often reverse, and it is the child worrying about what will happen to his parent if the child were not present to see to the care of the aging parent. Even pet lovers worry about what will happen to their pet should the owner no longer be around.

There is little that can be done to prepare those who depend on you for the loss of your companionship and emotional support; but there are many things you can do to provide financial support for those who rely on you. Even people of modest means can make financial provision so their loved ones will have an easy transition from being dependent to becoming self sufficient.

This chapter explains the many simple, and relatively inexpensive, things you can do to provide care for your loved ones should you not be present to do so yourself.

PROVIDING FOR THE MINOR CHILD

It doesn't happen very often, but both parents could die or become incapacitated before their child reaches adulthood. Most parents don't want to think about, much-less prepare for such a happening. But in this age of postponed parenthood, many parents are having children in their thirties and forties, and find themselves raising children into their fifties and sixties. The probability of a life threatening illness increases with age, so parents need to understand the importance of planning ahead. Regardless of the parent's age, planning for the care of a minor child should be part of every parent's Estate Plan, not only because it is the responsible thing to do, but also because it is easy to do and can be done at little cost.

CARING FOR THE PERSON OF THE CHILD

A child must be cared for in two ways, the *person* of the child and the *estate* (the property) of the child. To care for the person of the child, someone must be in charge of the child's everyday living, not only food and shelter but to provide social, ethical and religious training. Someone must have legal authority to make medical decisions and see to the child's education. If both parents are unable to care for the person of a minor, the Probate court will appoint someone to serve as the child's Guardian until the child 's 18th birthday.

The Court may have the Guardian care for the child's property, but if the child's assets are significant the Court may decide to appoint a Conservator to take charge of the child's property left to the child. The Conservator will be responsible to see that sufficient monies are used for the care of the child and that anything left over is preserved until the child becomes an adult.

APPOINTING A GUARDIAN FOR YOUR CHILD

If one parent dies, then it is the right, and duty, of the surviving parent to care for the child. But it could happen that both parents become incapacitated or die before the child is grown. In Michigan, parents have the right to appoint someone to care for their child in the event that neither of them are able to do so.

A parent can appoint someone to serve as the Guardian of their minor child by Will or by signing a separate document in the presence of two witnesses. If a parent names a Guardian and there is no surviving parent or if the surviving parent is unable to care for the child, then the appointment becomes effective as soon as the Guardian files an acceptance of the appointment with the Probate court. The Guardian needs to notify the child and the child's nearest adult relative of the acceptance. If the child is at least 14 years of age, the child can prevent the appointment by filing a written objection with the Court within 28 days of the acceptance. The child has the right to choose his own Guardian, subject to the approval of the Court (MCL 700.5202, 700.5203).

The child's Guardian can receive money payable for the child's support. If the Guardian receives more money than is needed, then the Guardian has the duty to save the excess for the child's future needs. If the child stands to inherit a significant amount of money, the Court may decided to appoint a Conservator for those funds (MCL 700.5215).

LEAVING PROPERTY FOR THE CHILD

As any parent is well aware, it is expensive to raise a child. People that you might consider to be the best choice to serve as your child's Guardian might not be able to do so unless you leave sufficient monies to pay for the care of the child. If you are a person of limited finances, then consider purchasing a term life insurance policy on your life and/or on the life of the other parent of the child. If you can only afford one policy, then insure the life of the parent who contributes most to the support of the child.

Term insurance policies are relatively inexpensive if you limit the term to just that period of time until your child becomes an adult. Some companies offer a combination of term life and disability insurance. As with any other purchase, it is important to comparison shop to obtain the best price for the coverage.

Parents often name their spouse as the primary beneficiary of their life insurance policy, and name their child as an alternate beneficiary. Married or single you can name your child as the primary beneficiary of the policy. If the child is a minor at the time the life insurance proceeds are to be distributed, and the value of the policy is not greater than $10,000, then under Michigan law, the company can distribute the funds to an adult member of the child's family or to a trust company. If the value of the policy is more than $10,000, the company will require Court approval before transferring the funds (MCL 554.531). The Court will appoint someone (usually the child's surviving parent) to serve as Conservator of the child's property until the child is 18.

Conservatorship procedures are expensive to set up and maintain. If the surviving parent is responsible and able to care for the child, then it is important to avoid the need to appoint a Conservator. A Trust is the best solution, but if finances are limited, then a good alternative is to appoint someone to serve as a Custodian of the funds under the Michigan Uniform Transfers to Minors Act.

THE MICHIGAN UNIFORM TRANSFERS TO MINORS ACT

The Michigan Uniform Transfers to Minors Act is designed to protect gifts made to a minor. It is appropriate to use this method if you want to give a child a gift of a security (stock or bond), or a life insurance policy, real property, or even tangible property such as an expensive painting.

Once the gift is made it becomes irrevocable, so this method is not appropriate unless you are sure that you want the child to have the gift once he/she is an adult. Also, the gift can be made only to one child. If you wish to make a gift to two children, then you will need to make a separate gift to each of them.

To make a gift under the Michigan Uniform Transfers to Minors Act, you need to name a trusted relative or friend or even a financial institution to be the Custodian of the gift. For example, if you wish to make a gift of stock, with a financial institution as Custodian, then the owner of the policy can be listed as:

"ABC BANK as custodian for _____ (name of minor) under the Michigan Uniform Transfers to Minors Act."

Although the gift is irrevocable, your choice of Custodian is not. If you later want to change from the ABC BANK to another person or institution, you are free to do so (MCL 554.527, 554.533, 554.535, 554.546).

You can include the Michigan Transfers to Minors Act as part of your Will. You can name someone to be Custodian to care for the gift until the child reaches 18. You can extend that time up to age 21 by specifying the age in your Will. Should you die after the child's designated birthday, the Personal Representative will give the gift to the child. If you die before the designated birthday, Custodian will take control of the property and keep it invested until it is time to distribute it to the child.

The Custodian has the discretion to use the gift to care for the child. The Custodian can pay monies directly to the child, or can use the money for the child's benefit. The Custodian can refuse to use any of the monies for the child and just keep the property or funds invested until it is time to distribute the property. If the Custodian wants to keep the funds invested, the child's Guardian, or even the child once he/she is 14, can ask the Probate Court to give a full accounting of the funds and then order the Custodian to part with some or all of the money. The Judge will decide what is in the child's best interest and then rule on the matter (MCL 554.537, 554.539, 554.540, 554.545, 554.546, 554.547).

The Custodian needs to invest and manage the property in a responsible, prudent manner. He is entitled to be paid for his effort. If the gift is sizeable, then the Custodian's fee can be sizeable. Before appointing a person or a company as Custodian, it is best to come to a written agreement about what will be charged to manage the custodial property.

☎ LAWYER | A TRUST FOR THE CHILD

If you have sufficient monies to care for your child until adulthood, then consult with an attorney about setting up a Trust for the child or drafting a Will with a trust provision to care for the child should you die before the child is grown. The only problem with having a Trust included in your Will is that the Trust is funded by your Probate Estate; and as such may increase the cost of probate as well as the cost of administering the Trust. If you have a significant amount of money, the better route might be to set up a Revocable Living Trust. You can fund the Trust while you are alive and bypass probate altogether.

The person you name as Trustee will handle the Trust funds should you die before the child reaches maturity. You can name the other parent as your Trustee, or if you wish, you can appoint a financial institution to manage the Trust funds. If you do not appoint the other parent as Trustee, then that parent still has the right, and duty, to care for the child. If you instruct the Trustee to use Trust funds for the child's support and maintenance, then the Trustee can set up a payment schedule with the child's parent to use the funds for everyday necessities. If you instruct the Trustee to keep all of the funds invested until the child reaches maturity, then the Trustee will do so and distribute the Trust funds directly to the child at whatever age you specify in the Trust document.

As with any fiduciary, the Trustee is entitled to be paid a reasonable fee. Before appointing a Trustee, you need to determine what it will cost to manage the Trust.

PROVIDING FOR THE STEPCHILD

Perhaps the reason that the story of Cinderella has such universal appeal is that many stepchildren, at one point or another, feel left out. The law seems to reinforce that perception. If you have a stepchild and your spouse die, then you, and not your stepchild, have the authority to agree to an anatomical gift (see Page 5). If all of your spouse's property is held jointly with you, then should your spouse die first, your stepchild will be left nothing.

Of course giving you the right to inherit all of your spouse's estate must be a decision that is agreeable to your spouse. If your spouse wants your step-child to inherit property, then your spouse can arrange his/her finances so that the child will inherit property. Hopefully, your spouse will consult with an estate planning attorney who can explain the best way to achieve that goal, else that intent could be thwarted and the child end up with less than your spouse intended as was the case in the example given on page 123.

Also, your spouse has the choice of giving your stepchild the right to make medical decisions and manage your spouse's finances. Your spouse could elect to appoint his/her child as a Patient Advocate to make medical decisions in the event that your spouse is unable to do so. And your spouse could arrange his/her finances to give your stepchild authority to manage your spouse's property in the event that your spouse is unable to do so.

The stepparent often comes across as villain, but it is the parent, and not the stepparent, who decides whether to allow the child's input on medical and financial decisions. And it is the parent, not the stepparent, who decides whether the child shall inherit property belonging to the parent.

THE SECOND MARRIAGE TRUST

A relatively simple solution to the problem of providing for children of a prior marriage is to have a Trust prepared. If you have minor children from a prior marriage, your can have a Trust prepared that will provide funds to care for the children till grown, and at that time, the monies be distributed to your surviving spouse and children in whatever manner you wish. If your children are grown, you may want the income of the Trust to be used to support your surviving spouse; and once the spouse dies, the remainder distributed to your children. A properly drafted Trust can provide for the care of your spouse and child in what ever way you think best.

That was the case with an elderly widower who married a pretty girl one quarter of his age. Their Pre-nuptial Agreement made it clear that all his property would go to his son from his first marriage. Surprisingly, the marriage turned out well. So well that the couple had two daughters. The husband decided to divide his estate equally between his three children and to provide for the care of his wife until the youngest child was grown.

His attorney suggested a Trust. "You can be Trustee during your lifetime. Once you die, your successor Trustee can immediately distribute one-third of the Trust to your son who is now 55. No need to keep him waiting. The rest of your money can remain in your Trust. Income from the Trust can be used to support your wife and children until the youngest is 25. Then, whatever remains in the Trust can be distributed equally to your daughters."

"Good idea" said the elderly gentlemen, with a smile "Just make sure it is revocable during my lifetime. Who knows what adventures I might be up to in the future?"

It isn't just stepchildren who can be left out if no provision is made. Even children from a long-standing marriage can be cut off against the wishes of a parent. A parent may assume that all of their children will be treated equally once both parents are gone, but if all their property is held jointly, the last parent to die is the one who gets to decide "who gets what." Too often, the wishes of the deceased parent are ignored, for example:

THE STRAINED RELATIONSHIP: A child may have a close relationship with one parent, and a strained, but tolerable, relationship with the other. Peace in the family is achieved because the parent who is close to the child acts as a buffer. Should the buffer parent die first, then the relationship between the surviving parent and the child may fall apart altogether and the child's inheritance be cut off.

THE PARENT WITH DIMINISHED CAPACITY: The more common scenario, is that the surviving parent becomes increasingly dependent on one child — either for emotional support, or for physical assistance as the parent ages. The other children may live at a distance, or perhaps they are too involved with their own family to assist. The supporting child may end up with most, if not all, of what was intended for all of the children.

These problems can be avoided by having your attorney prepare a Family Trust. The family assets are placed in the Trust with the parents as co-Trustees. The beneficiaries of the Trust cannot be changed unless both parents agree to the change. Once one parent dies, the Trust becomes irrevocable. The Trust income goes to the surviving parent and once that parent dies, whatever remains in the Trust is distributed in the manner as was agreed by both parents.

CARING FOR THE CARETAKER

If you are the caretaker of someone who is incapacitated, then in addition to preparing your own Estate Plan, you need to be concerned about who will care for the incapacitated person should something happen to you. Someone will need to make medical decisions for the incapacitated person and see to it that he/she is properly housed and fed. Often a family member agrees to take responsibility for the care of an incapacitated person in the event that the caretaker dies. But perhaps no one wants the job, or the opposite case, too many want to have control. For example, if a parent is incapacitated, one child may want the parent to remain at home with the assistance of a home health care worker. Another child may think the best place for the parent is an assisted living facility with 24 hour care. The caretaker spouse may be concerned that a tug-of-war will erupt once he dies.

In such case, the caretaker spouse should consult with an attorney to ensure future care for the incapacitated spouse. The attorney may suggest that a Guardian be appointed for the incapacitated spouse while the caretaker is alive. Once the guardianship is in place, the court will continue to supervise the care of the incapacitated person until he/she is restored to capacity or dies.

The Guardian-spouse has the right to choose a successor Guardian either in his Will or by means of a separate writing. Should the Guardian-spouse die before the Ward, then the successor Guardian can agree to serve as Guardian. Before accepting the appointment the successor must give notice to whoever is caring for the incapacitated person, or to the nearest adult relative. Should anyone object to the appointment, the Court will have a hearing and then decide who shall serve as Guardian (MCL 700.5301).

 **LAWYER**

A SPECIAL NEEDS TRUST
FOR THE INCAPACITATED

If a person is incapacitated, both the federal and state government provide assistance with programs such as social security disability benefits and custodial nursing home care under the Medicaid program. The family often supplements the government program by providing for the incapacitated person's *special needs*, such as clothing, hobbies, special education, outings to a movie or a sports event — things that give the incapacitated person some quality of life.

To be eligible for government assistance programs the incapacitated must be essentially without funds. Caretakers fear that leaving money to the incapacitated in a Will or Trust will disqualify the incapacitated from further government assistance. Understanding this dilemma, the federal government allow a parent, grandparent or legal guardian to set up a *Medicaid Special Needs Trust* as authorized by 42 U.S.C. 1396(d)(4) with the incapacitated as the beneficiary of the Trust.

The statute allows the Trustee to use Trust funds to provide for the special needs of the incapacitated. If any funds remain in the Special Needs Trust after the incapacitated dies, then those monies must be used to reimburse the state for monies spent on behalf of the incapacitated person.

An experienced Elder Law attorney can explain the different options available to the family to continue to provide for the incapacitated person's special needs in the event that the caretaker family member dies.

CARING FOR YOUR PET

A woman died at peace,
leaving her fortune
and care of her cat to her niece.
Alas, the fortune and the cat
Soon disappeared after that.

You could leave money to someone with the understanding that the person will take care of your pet, but the moral of the above limerick, is that just leaving money will not guarantee care for your pet.

 ## TRUST FOR CARE OF PET

A Pet Trust is valid under Michigan statute, so if you are financially able, you can employ an attorney to set up a Trust for the care of your pet, or you can have the attorney include a Trust provision for your pet in your Will (MCL 700.2722)

The person you name as Trustee will be charged with the duty to use Trust funds to pay for the care of your pet. You also need to name a remainder beneficiary (a person or perhaps a charitable organization) to receive whatever remains in the Trust after the pet dies. If you intend the Trustee to also serve as custodian of your pet, then you can ask the remainder beneficiary to regularly check to see to it that your pet is treated humanely, if not benevolently.

If you don't have the resources to set up a Trust to care for your pet, you can still ask a fellow pet lover to care for the animal. If no one among your circle of family and friends is able to do so, ask your pet's veterinarian to consider starting an "Orphaned Pet Service" to assist in finding new homes for pets who lose their owners. It is good public relations and a potential source of income. If this is agreeable to the Veterinarian, you can make arrangements in your Will to pay the Vet to care for the pet until a suitable family can be found. This is a more humane approach than the, all too common practice, of putting a pet "to sleep" rather than have the pet suffer the loss of its master. And in at least one case, that reasoning backfired.

Eleanor always had a pet in the house. After her husband died, her two poodles were her constant companions. When Eleanor became ill with cancer, she worried about what would happen to her "buddies" if she died. She finally decided it best to have her family put them to sleep when she died.

Eleanor endured surgery, chemotherapy, radiation therapy, and even some holistic remedies, but she continued to go downhill. Eleanor's family came in to visit her at the hospital to say their last good-byes. She was so ill, she didn't even recognize them. No one thought she could last the day. Because the family was from out of state, and time short, they decided to put the pets to sleep so they need only take care of the funeral arrangements when she died.

To everyone's surprise, Eleanor rallied. She lived two more long, lonely years.

She often said she wished they had put her to sleep instead of her buddies.

ARRANGING TO PAY BILLS

When people think about their estate plan they are more concerned about giving their possessions away than thinking about paying bills. If you are the breadwinner of the family, then you need to think about how your family will manage without you. Eventually, all who are dependent on you will need to fend for themselves, but there are things you can do to help them through the transition period until they become self sufficient.

First and foremost is to consider how monies you owe will be paid. If you don't give this some serious thought, then your estate could be quickly depleted. Even people who have no dependents need to give this some thought. If not, then all the heirs may inherit is a bunch of unpaid bills. This was the case with Larry. He had no family to speak of. After his wife died, he bought a condominium in Bay City. Over the years, he developed a close network of friends. They became his family. Larry did not have much money. He had a mortgage on the condominium. His car was leased. But he wanted his friends to know how much they meant to him so he had a Will drafted giving all he owned to five close friends.

The friends appreciated the gesture but the inheritance turned out to be a nightmare. They had to keep current the mortgage payments and the maintenance fees until the condominium was sold. Because Larry left little cash, this money had to come out of the beneficiaries' pockets. Two were living on their social security income and they had to borrow money from the others to contribute to their share of the upkeep.

The beneficiaries had no money to settle the lease on the car. Even if they did, they decided that there was no point in doing so because the amount needed to obtain clear title was greater than the current market value of the car. The beneficiaries decided not to make any further payment and they returned the car to the leasing agent. Their decision turned out to be a losing proposition. The leasing agent took the car, sold it and then sued the estate for the balance of the monies owed on the lease.

Because the beneficiaries had to quickly liquidate the estate, the condominium sold for less than it would have had they the time, energy and resources to fix it up. After they settled with the leasing agent, paid off the funeral expenses, mortgage, and probate fees there was only a few hundred dollars left. That was a lot of work and stress for nothing.

The pity was that Larry could have arranged his finances so that his beneficiaries were not burdened by his debt. He could have taken out mortgage insurance as part of the loan package. In most cases the cost of the insurance is nominal and is included as part of the monthly mortgage payment.

Larry could have done the same when he leased the car. Most leasing contracts offer term life insurance as an option. The cost of such insurance depends on the age of the person, the term of the loan and the amount of monies owed, but the premium paid each month is just a small fraction of the loan payment.

Even if Larry just arranged for payment of one of these debts, his beneficiaries would have come away with the gift that Larry intended, instead of the headache that they inherited.

PROVIDE FOR CREDIT CARD DEBT

If you have significant credit card debt, you need to consider how that debt will be paid once you die. Most credit card companies offer insurance policies and include the premium as part of your monthly payment. If you have such insurance, then should you die, any outstanding balance is paid. It benefits the credit card company to offer life insurance as part of the credit package, because they are assured of prompt payment should the borrower die. However, if you have little or no assets and no one other than yourself is liable to pay the debt, you may have no incentive to pay for insurance that can only benefit the lender.

As discussed in Chapters 2 and 4, if you hold a credit card jointly with another person, both of you are equally liable to pay the debt. If one of you dies, the other is responsible to pay the bill regardless of who ran up the bill. If paying that bill could be a struggle for the surviving debtor, then the better route to go is for each of you to have your own credit card.

Still another reason not to hold a joint credit card is that each of you can establish your own line of credit. This is especially important if you are married and one of you is retired or has been out of the job market for any period of time. Should the breadwinner die, it may be difficult for the surviving partner to establish credit if he/she has no recent work record. It is easier for the unemployed spouse to establish a line of credit when he/she is married to someone who is working.

PURCHASE LIFE INSURANCE

The good part of purchasing loan insurance — be it credit card insurance, mortgage insurance or car insurance, is that you can usually purchase the insurance without taking a medical examination. The down side is that such insurance may be more expensive than a life insurance policy. If you are in fairly good health, consider taking out a life insurance policy to cover all of your outstanding loans. The cost of the single life insurance policy may be significantly less than purchasing separate loan insurance policies.

The estate planning strategy of purchasing life insurance to pay off all of your loans works best if you are married and your spouse is jointly liable for your debts. If you name your spouse as beneficiary of the life insurance policy, then he/she can use the life insurance funds to pay off all monies owed. If you name your spouse or child and that person has no legal obligation to pay your debts, and if your primary residence is in Michigan, then none of your creditors can force your beneficiary to use any part of those funds to pay your debts, unless you purchased the insurance policy to defraud your creditors. If your creditor can proof that such was your intent, then the creditor can require that whatever you paid to purchase the policy, plus interest, be subtracted from the proceeds and be used to pay your debt (MCL 500.2207).

If you want the insurance funds used to pay your debts, then leaving the money to someone who has no duty to pay the debt is not the way to go. But, if you want to be sure that someone receives money for their care after you are gone, then purchasing life insurance should accomplish your goal.

With or without debt, you may be wondering about life insurance — should you have it? How much is enough? The answer to these questions depends on the "sleep at night" factor, namely how much insurance do you need to make you not worry about insurance coverage when you go to sleep at night? It is often more an emotional than a financial issue.

Some people have an "every man for himself" attitude and are content to have no life insurance at all. When they die, whatever they have, they have. And that is what their heirs will inherit. Others worry about how their loved ones will manage if they are not around to support them, and decide to purchase enough insurance to maintain their dependents in their accustomed life style.

The same person may have different thoughts about insurance coverage as the circumstances of their life changes — from no coverage in their bachelor days to more-than-enough coverage in their child rearing days to just-enough-to-bury-me in their senior years.

Insurance companies recognize that people's needs change over the years. Many companies offer flexible insurance coverage. As with any consumer item, it is a good idea to shop around.

PROVIDING FOR THE FAMILY BUSINESS

If you are the sole proprietor of a business, then you need to give considerable thought to what will happen to that business in the event of your incapacity or death. Can the business continue to operate without you? Is it your intent that whoever inherits your business take over its daily operations or do you think it best to have the business sold and have the proceeds of the sale given to your beneficiaries? If you do not make provision for the orderly transfer of your business, then your Personal Representative or a Probate Court may need to make that decision for you.

In addition to the running of the business you need to consider how company debts will be paid. If your business is highly leveraged (business talk for "owes lots of money"), you also need to consider how those loans will be paid should you become disabled or die.

Taxes are still another concern. Your business may be worth millions on paper, and your estate taxes will be based on that value. You heirs may be forced to sell the company just to pay the taxes, but without your leadership they may get only a fraction of the value of the company. A solution to the problem is to purchase a key man or life insurance policy to pay taxes and get the company through the transition period.

An attorney or a financial planner who is experienced in business matters can offer other suggestions as to the best method of ensuring that the business continues its operation, or terminates in an orderly fashion — whichever is applicable in your case.

ESTATE PLANNING FOR THE BANKRUPT

You may think the above title to be an oxymoron (a contradiction in terms). If a person is bankrupt, why plan for an estate he doesn't have? But facts are, that people who file for bankruptcy are often quite wealthy and that is their downfall. Because they have substantial income or property, banks and people are willing to lend them money. If more money is borrowed than can be repaid, the unhappy result is bankruptcy. In the event that you are concerned about meeting your responsibilities as parent or spouse, yet you enjoy a life style of financial brinksmanship, then consider investing in items that are "creditor proof."

That's exactly what Alan decided to do. Alan was an astute man, well aware of his strengths and weaknesses. He was a sharp businessman, someone who enjoyed his work and who knew he had the capacity to earn large sums of money. But he also knew he was a gambler. Not the Las Vegas type, but a gambler in business ventures. "No risk, no gain" was his favorite saying.

If you charted his net worth over the years it would look like the peaks and valleys of the NASDAQ. Lots of high highs and lots of low lows. Unfortunately, he married a woman who did not share his adventurous spirit. His wife became increasingly intolerant of their financial instability. She came to realize that this was his life style and things would never change. "All gamblers die broke," she said as she walked out the door with their 5 year old daughter in tow.

That, and the fact that he had to declare bankruptcy, brought Alan up short; and he began to be concerned about his future and that of his family.

Alan talked things over with his bankruptcy attorney "I am a good businessman, but not a clairvoyant. There was no way to predict the turn of events that led to this situation. But I know I will bounce back, and it will just be a matter of time before I am earning a good living. I also know that I am an entrepreneur and not a 9 to 5 type guy. This could happen again. What concerns me is how to provide security for my child in the event that something happens to me before she is grown."

His attorney answered "Buying a homestead is a good investment to make sure your wife and child have a roof over their heads. You might consider holding all of your bank accounts jointly with your spouse or child. Just be sure that the account is held jointly with right of survivorship and not as a Statutory Joint Account. Your family member can take a joint account with right of survivorship free of the claims of your creditors, but by Michigan law, your share of a Statutory Joint Account is available to pay your debts."

The attorney continued "You can purchase life insurance making your wife or child beneficiary. They will inherit the proceeds free of your debts. I don't recommend that you purchase a policy at this time. Should you buy the policy now that you are insolvent (i.e., you owe more than you own), then should you die, any of your creditors can demand that the money you paid for the policy (plus interest) be given to them and not to your beneficiary. But only the premium (what you paid) is at risk. If the premium is just a small part of the proceeds, then consider life insurance as part of your Estate Plan. These are simple Estate Planning strategies. When you are ready to do some serious Estate Planning, we can get together and discuss more sophisticated strategies."

ANNUITIES TO SPREAD THE INHERITANCE

It is not uncommon for an heir go through his inheritance within two years. For many, the reason the money is gone so soon, is that there just wasn't much money to inherit in the first place. But for others, it's a spending frenzy. You probably know your family well enough to know whether your intended beneficiary is a squirrel, always saving for the winter or whether it is their life style to Earn-A-Penny Spend-A-Penny.

If you want to leave an insurance policy benefit to someone you love, but the intended beneficiary is immature, or a born spendthrift, then a simple solution to the problem may be to purchase an annuity rather than life insurance. An annuity is a type of insurance policy that can be set up so that your beneficiary (the **annuitant**) receives money on a monthly, or yearly basis, rather than a single lump sum payment when you die.

An annuity can also be set up to benefit your favorite charity, and to reduce, if not eliminate the Capital Gains Tax. For example, suppose you own several acres of land in Maine that you purchased many years ago. You may have been putting off selling the property because of the Capital Gains Tax. But it has been a liability to you. It produces no income and because the property continues to appreciate, each year, you are paying more and more in property taxes. If you are living on a pension income, it makes no sense to continue to pay money in property taxes, when that money could be used to give you additional income. A solution to the problem may be to donate the property to your favorite charity with an agreement that they will sell the property and use the money to purchase an annuity that will give you an income for your life. The agreement is called the **Charitable Remainder Annuity Trust**.

THE CHARITABLE REMAINDER ANNUITY TRUST

A Charitable Remainder Annuity Trust is a Trust that is established according to the Internal Revenue Code (IRC 664). Charities do not pay taxes, so property donated to the Trust can be sold by the Trustee free of the Capital Gains Tax. The money from the sale is invested so that it provides an income (an annuity) to you either for a fixed period of time, say 20 years, or for your lifetime as computed by actuarial tables (i.e., your estimated life expectancy). It can even be set up so that the annuity continues to be paid to your spouse after your death.

How much income you receive depends on the value of the donated property and the length of time that the annuity is paid. Your financial planner or Estate Planning attorney can suggest the type of Charitable Trust that best meets your Estate Planning goals.

Of course there is always the downside and Charitable Remainder Annuity Trust is no exception. It may cost significant attorney fees to set up the Trust. Some charities may offer to have their attorney prepare the Trust at no cost to you, or perhaps they offer a "standard" Trust document that their attorney prepared. But using their Trust document represents a conflict of interest. Their Trust was prepared by an attorney for the greatest benefit to his client (that's the charity, not you). It is important that you employ your own attorney to represent you. He knows the extent of your Estate and he understands what you wish to accomplish. Once established, the Trust is irrevocable, so it is important that you understand all of the aspects of the Trust, including what income taxes will need to be paid by the annuitant.

If you decide to set up a Charitable Remainder Annuity Trust, then the benefits to you are many:

☑ TAX SAVINGS

Had you sold the property and invested the money yourself, you would have had to pay a Capital Gains Tax and that tax could be substantial, depending on the tax rate in effect at the time of the transfer. By gifting the property the full value of the land can be used to produce investment income.

You will no longer need to pay annual property taxes. And you even get to take a charitable deduction on your income tax return in the year the gift is made.

☑ NO PROBATE EXPENSE

Because the land is in a different state, it could be both time consuming and expensive to transfer the property to your beneficiaries upon your death. By donating the property to the Trust, you avoid the need for a Probate procedure in another state.

☑ CREDITOR PROTECTION

If you keep the land and are sued, you could lose it to pay your creditors. If your spouse inherited the land, it could be lost to creditors. But once the property is transferred into the Trust, the gift is made. Neither your creditors nor the creditors of any successor annuitant of the Trust can get access to the Trust property. The most the creditor can do is ask for payment from the money received as an income.

☑ SPENDTHRIFT PROVISION

If your spouse is a spendthrift and inherited the land, all of the money could be spent in short order. You can set up this annuity Trust for the benefit of your spouse and be assured that your spouse will have a steady income over a long period of time.

☑ GIVE WHEN NEEDED INSTEAD OF LATER

A Charitable Remainder Annuity Trust can be set up in any number of different ways to accommodate your Estate Plan. For example, if you are not in need of a present income, but expect that you will spend significant sums on your child's education, you can set up a 20 year annuity with your child as the annuitant. This will get the child through college and probably be a great help in should the child decide to start a family. Why have the child inherit property in later, high earning years rather than in the early, high expense/low income years?

☑ GOOD DEED

Whatever is left of the donation after payment of the annuity goes to your favorite charity. By making a donation to the charity of your choice, you are sharing your good fortune with others. You can consider this as "giving back" to the community, or just plain doing a good deed.

A Health Care Estate Plan 10

The last two chapters discussed the distribution or management of your estate once you are deceased. But in this age of an extended life expectancy, a more important topic is how to manage and preserve your estate in the event of a debilitating illness. As life expectancy increases, so does the percentage of the population who suffer incapacity from debilitating strokes, Alzheimer's disease or Parkinsons' disease. It is estimated that more than 50% of the population who are 85 or older, suffer some degree of dementia. Your best estate plan could be sabotaged by lengthy or incapacitating illness.

A *Health Care Estate Plan* is a plan designed to care for your person and property in the event of an incapacitating illness. In Chapter 7 we discussed how you can appoint a Patient Advocate to make your medical decisions in the event that you are too ill to do so yourself (see Page 168). Your Patient Advocate will care for your person in the event of your incapacity. But there is still the problem of who will care for your property.

In this chapter we will discuss how you can appoint someone to handle your finances in the event of your incapacity, and how you can arrange to pay for the health care that you may require as you age.

A TRUST TO CARE FOR PROPERTY

The optimum way to provide for the care of your property in the event of your incapacity, is to set up a Trust appointing a Successor Trustee to care for your property according to the directions given in your Trust. You can be Trustee of the funds while you have capacity. Should you become incapacitated, then the person you name as Successor Trustee will take over. If you are a person of substance, then you should consider having an attorney design a Trust especially for you.

You may be wondering what we mean by the term "a person of substance." We have avoided defining the term because wealth is a state of mind. If you think back on your life, you can probably recall times of well being, where you felt on top of the world and a fortunate person. Excluding winners of game shows and the lottery, for most of us, the moment we felt most wealthy did not coincide with the high point of our net worth.

Except for the extremes of Bill Gates and a homeless person, whether you are poor or wealthy depends more on your subjective perception than any objective standard. Using this subjective standard, you should have a Trust prepared when you feel rich enough to conclude that the benefits of a Trust justify the cost of preparing and maintaining the Trust. And just to keep things grounded in reality, take an objective view of your finances by determining your *Net Worth* (the cash value of your assets, less the amount of monies you owe).

You can use the form on the next page to calculate that value. If you are married and hold all property jointly, then calculate the Net Worth of all of the assets and divide by 2, for your own Net Worth.

DETERMINING YOUR NET WORTH

ASSETS:

$_____ Cash (coin collection, bank accounts,
                        certificates of deposit, etc.)

$_____ Securities (stocks, bonds, mutuals, etc.)

$_____ Cash value of insurance policies

$_____ Pension Plans, IRA's, etc.

$_____ Cash value of a partnership or other
                        business interest

$_____ Tangible personal property (jewelry,
                        private art or stamp collections,
                        motor vehicles, etc.)

$_____ Real property (residences, vacant
                        lots, condominiums, cooperatives,
                        time shares, etc.)

$_____ TOTAL VALUE OF ASSETS

It may be that you and the bank own all of this, so you
need to subtract away monies that you owe on any of
the above items:

LIABILITIES

$_____ Private loans
$_____ Mortgage Balance
$_____ Credit card debt
$_____ Car loan or car lease balance
$_____ TOTAL LIABILITIES

A simple subtraction gives you your *net worth*:
ASSETS — LIABILITIES = NET WORTH

THE CONVENIENCE ACCOUNT

If you do not have sufficient assets to justify the cost of employing an attorney to draft a Trust, and you are concerned that at some time in the future you may become incapacitated and unable to handle your finances, then there are strategies, other than a Trust, that you can use to solve the problem.

THE CONVENIENCE ACCOUNT

You can set up your checking account so that a trusted family member can write checks on the account. Of course there are all the inherent problems of a joint account that we discussed on page 177. You can avoid many of those problems by limiting the amount of money that can be accessed by the family member. For example, you can arrange your finances so that all of your bills are paid from a single checking account and your family member can access that account, only.

If you set up a joint account, your family member will own whatever is in the account should your die. If this is not as you wish, you can instruct the bank that this is a convenience account and that in the event of your death the family member may no longer access your account. If you are setting up a Statutory Joint Account, then all you need do is check the appropriate spaces stating that the funds in the account go to your estate when you die (MCL 487.715).

But ultimately the family member must be trustworthy because the bank is under no duty to stop your family member from writing checks on your account until the Bank learns of your death.

AVOIDING GUARDIANSHIP

The joint or convenience account solves the problem of how to pay your bills in the event you are temporarily ill. It does not solve the problem of how to manage your business affairs in the event of an extended illness. For example, suppose you have a stroke and can no longer be cared for at home. Should it be necessary for you to sell your home and move to an assisted living facility, then no one will have the authority to sell the house for you. In such case, the Court will need to appoint a Conservator to transact business on your behalf, and probably a Guardian to make your medical decisions.

Conservator and guardianship procedures are expensive to set up and maintain. Curious that so many people worry about how to avoid Probate, when the larger concern should be how to avoid guardianship. Consider that it is not all that hard to arrange your finances so that no Probate is necessary. The cost to administer your estate should be $0. Even with a full Probate procedure, the administration usually ends within a year.

Whatever it costs to Probate your estate is a one-time expense. Once monies are distributed to the beneficiaries, it is ended. Not so if you become incapacitated. It can cost thousands of dollars to set up the guardianship and/or conservatorship; and more money will be spent to care for you and your property each year. The Guardian and the Conservator (and their attorneys) are entitled to reasonable fees. Even if the same person serves as Guardian and Conservator, the charge to your Estate is sizeable. And this expense continues, year after year, until your are returned to capacity, or die. One way to avoid conservator procedures is to give someone authority to manage your affairs, should you become incapacitated. A Trust is the best vehicle. For those of limited means, a Power of Attorney is the next best estate plan.

A POWER OF ATTORNEY FOR FINANCES

A Power of Attorney is a legal document by which someone (the **Principal**) gives another (his **Agent** or **Attorney-In-Fact**) authority to do certain acts on behalf of the Principal. If you want someone to be able to conduct business on your behalf in the event of your incapacity, then you can make the Power of Attorney **durable** by adding the phrase "This Power of Attorney is not affected by the principal's subsequent disability or incapacity, or by the lapse of time." (MCL 700.5501).

You can give your Agent general powers to manage your finances, to do much the same with your property as you can do yourself, such as:

⇨   sell any of your real or personal property;

⇨   buy real or personal property for you;

⇨   trade in securities;

⇨   pay your bills and/or taxes;

⇨   operate your business;

⇨   have access to your safe deposit box;

⇨   borrow money on your behalf;

⇨   purchase insurance policies and name beneficiaries;

⇨   sue or defend a law suit on your behalf.

Or if you wish you can limit the things your Agent can do for you to just one or two things specifically authorized in your Power of Attorney.

Limited or general, the operative word in any Power of Attorney is POWER. Once your Agent has authority to act, he essentially steps in your shoes and can do whatever you gave him authority to do.

Your primary consideration in choosing an Agent is trustworthiness. You need to choose someone who will follow your instructions and put the Durable Power of Attorney to the use that you intended. You need to choose someone, who, when using the Durable Power of Attorney, will always put your interests ahead of his.

Perhaps you are less concerned with trustworthiness than the loss of your independence. You may want to give someone a Power of Attorney, but not until it is needed. This presents a dilemma. If you wait until it is needed, you may be too sick to sign the document. There are two possible solutions.

KEEP THE DOCUMENT IN YOUR POSSESSION

Before anyone (a bank, stockbroker, closing agent, etc.) will accept the Power of Attorney they will want to see the original document so that they are assured that your Attorney-In-Fact has authority to transact business on your behalf. If you keep the original document in your possession and not give anyone a copy, your Agent will not be able to act for you.

The only problem with this arrangement is that you need to make the document accessible to your Agent in the event of your incapacity. If your Agent is a trusted family member, then you can give your Agent the location of the document with instructions to take possession of the Financial Power of Attorney in the event of your incapacity.

THE SPRINGING POWER OF ATTORNEY

A better solution may be to have your attorney draft a "springing" Durable Power of Attorney that is not operational until your family doctor and/or independent physician says that you are incapacitated and unable to manage your financial affairs. Your Attorney-In-Fact can hold the original document, but cannot use it until it "springs to life" when a doctor determines that you are too ill to care for your property.

Whichever method you use, your Power of Attorney must be "*durable*," otherwise your Attorney-In-Fact will not have authority to act should you become incapacitated. And of course, the whole purpose of the document, is to have someone take care of your finances in the event you are too ill to do so yourself.

CARING FOR YOU WHEN YOU CAN'T

It is relatively simple and inexpensive to head off guardianship or conservatorship proceedings. All you need do is appoint an Agent under a Durable Power of Attorney to manage your finances, and a Patient Advocate to make your medical care decisions. These documents authorize people of your choice to care for you and your property in the event of your incapacity. But, despite your best plans, something unusual could happen causing a Court to decide that you need a Guardian or a Conservator. For example, suppose you disappear and cannot be found after a diligent search. It might be necessary to have a Court appoint a Conservator to protect your property in your absence. Or perhaps you develop an addiction or a mental illness causing self-destructive behavior. Your friends or family might decide that you are in need of protection and ask a Court determine whether you are incapacitated, i.e., unable to care for yourself, and if so, then to appoint a Guardian to care for you (MCL 700.5303).

Although it may not be possible to avoid all guardianship and conservatorship proceedings, you can have some measure of control in your fate by deciding who will care for you, provided you make that decision when you are well and have the capacity to do so. You can include a provision in your Durable Power of Attorney stating that should a Court find it necessary to appoint a Guardian or Conservator for you, then it is your desire that the Court appoint the person of your choice to serve. The Court will honor your choice, unless the person of your choice is not suitable to serve or is unwilling to do so (MCL 700.5313, 700.5409).

It is a good idea to choose the same person to serve as Guardian as you chose as Patient Advocate. If the Court appoints someone other than your Patient Advocate to be your Guardian, your Patient Advocate will continue to have the right to decide what medical treatment you should receive (MCL 700.5306). That could cause confusion or discord. For example, suppose your Guardian thinks you should be in nursing home, but your Advocate believes you would do better at home. The result could be an expensive court battle with the Judge making the final decision. And of course, the cost of that court battle comes out of your pocket.

Also, consider naming your Agent to serve as Conservator. Should the Court appoint someone, other than your Agent, to serve as Conservator, then the Conservator has the right to revoke your Durable Power of Attorney. If that happens, your Agent will have no further authority to act on your behalf (MCL 700.5503).

Although the probability of ever needing a Guardian or Conservator is small, it is important that you make your choice known. If not, then the Court gets to decide who will serve in these capacities. The Judge will give priority to your family members in the following order:

1st   Spouse, or a person chosen by your spouse.
2nd   Your adult child, or a person chosen by your child.
3rd   Your Parent or if deceased, anyone named in his/her Will to serve as your Conservator or Guardian.
4th   Any relative you have been living with for 6 months or more prior to the filing date of the petition to determine your capacity.

If no family member can serve, then whoever is caring for you or paying benefits for your care can make the choice (MCL 700.5313, 700.5409).

PAYING FOR LONG TERM CARE

The good news is: You are going to live longer.
The bad news is: It's going to cost you.

Scientists are doing a great job of prolonging life, but unless they find Ponce De Leon's fountain, the general population will age. Along with age comes infirmities. Eyes fail. Hearing diminishes. Nervous systems deteriorate. Digestive systems either speed up or slow down, all to the discomfort of the unhappy occupant of the body. It's all part of the "golden" years.

The pharmacology industry is well motivated to produce drugs that manage the ills associated with aging. Their research has led to a wealth of pharmaceutic products that do not cure, but do allow people to live relatively comfortably into advanced age. The only problem is the cost of these drugs. Medicare covers the treatment of life-threatening brushes with heart disease, stroke, cancer and diabetes; but, as of this writing, Medicare does not pay for maintenance medication that is often necessary once the condition is stabilized.

Medicare is also limited in long term health care coverage. It does not pay for extended nursing care. Medicare pays for the first 20 days of skilled nursing care. Medicare pays the excess over $99 for days 21 through 100. That means you pay $7,920 for the next 80 days. After 100 days, you are on your own. A nursing home stay of one or two years can wipe out the life savings of most working people. Once savings are gone, the government provides care in the form of Medicaid coverage.

If you are poor, long-term nursing care may not be of concern to you, because all your needs should be covered under Medicaid. If you are very wealthy, you may not worry because you have more than enough money to pay for your care. But the rest of us need to think about ways to provide for long-term health care.

For those concerned about the loss of life savings because of illness, there is supplemental and/or long-term health care insurance. There are many different insurance plans available. You can call the National Association of Insurance Commissioners at (816) 842-3600 and they will forward to you, free of charge, the publication:
    A SHOPPER'S GUIDE TO LONG TERM CARE INSURANCE

If you have a specific question, you can call the Michigan LONG TERM CARE HOTLINE at (800) 803-7174.

FOR FEDERAL EMPLOYEES
The Long Term Care Security Act (Public Law 106-265) was passed by the Congress to take effect in October, 2002. The law is designed to make long-term care insurance available to Federal employees, members of the uniformed services, and civilian and military retirees. The Office of Personnel Management is working to establishing the terms of the policy and cost to the federal employee or retiree. You can download a copy of the law from their Web site:

 OFFICE OF PERSONNEL MANAGEMENT
http://www.opm.gov/insure/ltc

The National Association Of Retired Federal Employees ("NARFE") has been actively involved in this new legislation. You can get updates on the law by calling their legislative hotline in Alexandria, Virginia at (703) 838-7780, or by visiting their Web site:

 NARFE WEB SITE
http://www.narfe.org

MEDICAID ESTATE PLANNING

Many people find themselves in the unhappy position of being uninsurable because of a pre-existing condition, or perhaps without sufficient income to pay for long term health insurance coverage. The worst case scenario is a person who has a serious illness and is too rich for Medicaid and too poor to afford nursing care without depleting his life savings.

People in this situation may decide to divest themselves of all property and hope that they will not need extended nursing care for at least three years. Once three years have passed, they hope to be eligible for Medicaid. For most, their motives are altruistic. The money is given to a child to keep safe for the parent, but what the parent is really trying to do is protect the child's inheritance.

The parent may rationalize: "I worked all my life and hoped to leave a few pennies for the kids. Why did I work so hard? To give it all to a nursing home? Why should I use all of my life savings to pay for a few years of nursing care? Doesn't the government pay hundreds of thousands of dollars for people on Medicare to have open heart surgery, or to pay for lengthy and expensive cancer treatments? Why should people who suffer from the effects of a severe stroke, or from Alzheimer's or from Parkinsons not be entitled to receive similar benefits for their disease?"

And so they give all of their money away.

Giving away all assets and then waiting three years is what this author considers to be a "Brute Force" Medicaid Estate Plan. There's no finesse. It is a drastic step to take and fraught with perils. The obvious problems are ones we mentioned before in connection with joint property.

What if the child is sued?

What if the child gets married, or divorced?

What if the child falls on hard times?

But the real problem is the loss of independence. Being impoverished at a time in your life when you are unable to supplement your income, and when your physical health is declining, can lead to much sadness. Imagine going to your child and asking for money. Imagine the child thinking, or worse yet, asking,

"What is the money for?"

Before divesting yourself of your assets, or if you are the child, before you accept those assets, consult with an experienced Elder Law attorney. In many cases, there are other, better, strategies.

 Medicaid Estate Planning is a specialty. The attorney must know all of the federal and state laws relating to the subject. In addition, the attorney needs to know what strategies are liable to be challenged should the person need to apply for Medicaid. Before employing an attorney, determine what percentage of his practice is devoted to Medicaid Estate Planning and how long he has practiced in the field of Elder Law.

Your Estate Plan Record 11

Once you are satisfied with your estate plan, then the final thing to consider is whether your heirs will be able to locate your assets once you are deceased.

Most people have their business records in one place, their Will in another place, car titles and deeds in still another place. When someone dies, their beneficiaries may feel as if they are playing a game of "hide and seek" with the decedent. The game might be fun if it were not for the fact that things not found may be forever lost. For example, suppose you die in an accident and no one knows you are insured by your credit card company for accidental death in the amount of $25,000. The only one to profit is the insurance company, which is just that much richer because no one told them that you died as a result of an accident.

And how about a key to a safe deposit box located in another state? Will anyone find it? Even if they find the key, how will they find the box?

It is not difficult to arrange things so that your affairs are always in order. It amounts to being aware of what you own (and owe) and keeping a record of your possessions. A side benefit is that by doing so, you will always know where all your business records are. If you ever spent time trying to collect information to file your taxes or trying to find a lost stock or bond certificate, you will appreciate the value of organizing your records.

Heirs need all the help they can get. It is difficult enough dealing with the loss, without the frustration of trying to locate important documents. Your heirs will have no problem locating your assets if you keep all of your records in a single place. It can be a desk drawer or a file cabinet or even a shoe box. It is helpful if you keep a separate file or folder for each type of investment. You might consider setting up the following folders:

 THE BANK & SECURITIES FOLDER

Store your original certificates for stocks, bonds, mutual funds, certificates of deposit, in a folder labeled **BANK & SECURITIES FOLDER**. In addition to the original certificate include a copy of the contract you signed with each financial institution. The contract will show where you have funds and who you named as beneficiary or joint owner of the account. If someone owes you money and has signed a Promissory note or mortgage that identifies you as the lender, then you can store these documents in this folder as well.

If you wish to store your original documents in a safe deposit box, then keep a record of the location of the safe deposit box, and the number of the box, in this folder. Make a copy of all of the items stored in the box and place the copies in this folder. If you have an extra key to the box, then put the key in the folder. If you are the only person with access to the box, it may take a probate procedure to remove items from the box once you die. Consider allowing someone you trust to be able to gain entry to the box in the event of your incapacity or death.

🗁 THE DEED FOLDER

Many people save every scrap of paper associated with the closing of real property. If you closed recently on real estate and there was a mortgage involved in the purchase, you probably walked away from closing with enough paper to wallpaper your kitchen. If you wish, you can keep all of those papers in a separate file that identifies the property, for example: CLOSING PAPERS FOR LANSING CONDO

Set aside the original deed (or a copy if the original is in a safe deposit box) and place it into a separate DEED FOLDER. Include deeds to parcels of real property, cemetery deeds, condominium deeds, cooperative shares to real property, timesharing certificates, etc. Include deeds to out of state property as well as Indiana property in the DEED FOLDER. If you have a mortgage on your property, then put a copy of the mortgage and promissory note in a separate LIABILITY FOLDER.

🗁 THE LIABILITY FOLDER

The LIABILITY FOLDER should contain all loan documents of debts that you owe. For example, if you purchased real property and have a mortgage on that property, then put a copy of the mortgage and promissory note in this folder. If you owe money on a car, put all of your loan documents in the file. If you have a credit card, put a copy of the contract you signed with the credit card company in this file. Many people never take the time to calculate their net worth (what a person owns less what that person owes). By having a record of your assets and outstanding debts, you can calculate your net worth whenever you wish.

📁 THE INSURANCE FOLDER

The INSURANCE FOLDER is for each original insurance policy that you own, be it car insurance, homeowner's insurance or a health care insurance policy. If you purchased real property, you probably received a title commitment at closing and the original title insurance policy some weeks later when you received your original deed from recording. If you cannot locate the title insurance policy, then contact the closing agent and have them send you a copy of your title policy.

📁 THE PENSION AND ANNUITY FOLDER

If you have a Pension or Annuity, then put all of the documents relating to the Pension in this folder. Include the telephone number and/or address of the person to contact in the event of your death.

FOR FEDERAL RETIREES If you are a Federal Retiree, you should have received your **PERSONAL IDENTIFICATION NUMBER (PIN)** and the person who will inherit your pension (your *survivor annuitant*) should have received his/her own PIN as well. It is relatively simple to obtain this during your lifetime, but it may be difficult and/or stressful for your survivor annuitant to work through the system once you are gone.

Survivor annuitant benefits are not automatic. Your survivor annuitant must apply for them by submitting a death claim to the Office of Personnel Management. Your survivor needs to know that it is necessary to apply and also how to apply. You can get printed information about how apply for benefits from the Office Of Personnel Management (see Page 30). Keep the printed information in this file.

🗁 THE PERSONAL PROPERTY FOLDER

MOTOR VEHICLES Put all motor vehicle titles in a Personal Property folder. This includes cars, mobile homes, boats, planes, etc. If you owe money on the vehicle, the lender may have possession of the title certificate. If such is the case, then put a copy of the title certificate and registration in this folder and a copy of the promissory note or chattel mortgage in a separate liability folder. If you have a boat or plane, then identify the location of the motor vehicle. For example, if you are leasing space in an airplane hanger or in a marina, keep a copy of the leasing agreement in this file.

JEWELRY If you own expensive jewelry, keep a picture of the item together with the sales receipt or written appraisal in this folder.

COLLECTOR'S ITEMS If you own a valuable art or coin collection, or any other item of significant value, include a picture of the item in this file. Also include evidence of ownership of the item, such as a sales receipt or a certificate of authenticity, or a written appraisal of the property.

🗁 THE ESTATE PLANNING DOCUMENT FOLDER

Place your Will and/or Trust in a separate folder. If the original document is in a safe deposit box, then place a copy of the document in this folder together with instructions about how to find the original. If you placed your Will with the Probate Court, then put the address of the Court in the folder together with a copy of the Will.

 THE TAX RECORD FOLDER

Your Personal Representative (or next of kin) will need to file your final income tax returns. Keep a copy of your tax returns (both Federal and state) for the past three years in your Tax Record Folder.

CAPITAL GAINS RECORD

As explained on page 37, as of 2010, there will be a cap on the step-up basis of inherited property of 4.3 million for property inherited by the spouse and 1.3 million for everyone else. It is important that you keep a careful record of the basis of your property, not only for your heirs, but yourself should you decide to sell the property during your lifetime. If you purchase a stock, then you need to keep a record of the money you paid for that stock. If you purchase real property, then you need to keep a record of the purchase price as well as monies you paid to improve the property. Your accountant can help you set up a bookkeeping system to keep a running record of your basis in everything you own of value.

THE PERSONAL RECORD FOLDER

The **PERSONAL RECORD FOLDER** should include documents that relate to you personally, such as a birth certificate, naturalization papers, pre-nuptial or post-nuptial agreement, marriage certificate, divorce papers, army records, social security card; etc. If you have a Patient Advocate Designation, or a Durable Power of Attorney, then this is a good place for these documents. If you placed the original document in a safe deposit box, keep a copy in this folder together with the location of the original.

Guiding Those Left Behind In Michigan

Each folder should contain a record of your ownership of the item and the location of that item. For example, if you own a vacant lot, your beneficiaries will find the deed (or a copy) in your DEED FOLDER, but that deed will not contain the address of that property because it doesn't have one. The post office does not assign a street address until someone actually lives at the site. Your beneficiary could get the location of the property from city or county records. But why make things hard for them, when a simple handwritten note can tell them exactly how to locate the property?

THE *If I Die* FILE

Many do not have the time, nor inclination, to "play" with all these folders. They do not anticipate an immediate demise. Getting hit by a truck, or dying in a fiery plane crash is not something to think about, much less prepare for. But consider that death is not the only problem. You could take suddenly ill (say with a stroke) and become incapacitated. Even the most time-starved optimist should have a murmur of concern that their loved ones will be left with a mess should something unforeseen happen.

If you do not feel like doing a complete job of organizing your records at this time, consider an abridged version. You can set up a single file with a list of all you own and the location of each item. You need to make that file easily accessible to whoever you wish to manage your affairs in the event of your incapacity or death. You can do this by letting that person know of the existence of the file and how to get it in an emergency; or keep the file in an easily accessed place in your home with the succinct but attention-grabbing title of "*If I Die*."

We have included a form on the next page that you can use as a basis for information to be included in the file.

If I Die

then the following information will help settle my estate:

INFORMATION FOR DEATH CERTIFICATE

MY FULL LEGAL NAME _____

MY SOCIAL SECURITY NO. _____

MY USUAL OCCUPATION _____

BIRTH DATE AND BIRTH PLACE _____

If naturalized, date & place _____

MY FATHER'S NAME _____

MY MOTHER'S MAIDEN NAME _____

PERSONS TO BE NOTIFIED OF MY DEATH

_____

_____

_____

FUNERAL AND BURIAL ARRANGEMENTS

LOCATION OF BURIAL SITE

_____

LOCATION OF PRENEED FUNERAL CONTRACT

_____

FOR VETERAN or SPOUSE BURIAL IN A NATIONAL CEMETERY

BRANCH_____SERIAL NO._____

VETERAN'S RANK _____

VETERAN'S VA CLAIM NUMBER _____

DATE AND PLACE OF ENTRY INTO SERVICE:

_____

DATE AND PLACE OF SEPARATION FROM SERVICE:

_____

LOCATION OF OFFICIAL MILITARY DISCHARGE
OR DD 214 FORM_____

LOCATION OF LEGAL DOCUMENTS

BIRTH CERTIFICATE _____

MARRIAGE CERTIFICATE _____

DIVORCE DECREE _____

PASSPORT _____

WILL OR TRUST _____

DEEDS _____

MORTGAGES _____

TITLE TO MOTOR VEHICLES _____

HEALTH CARE DIRECTIVES _____

Name, telephone of attorney _____

LOCATION OF FINANCIAL RECORDS

INSURANCE POLICIES:

Name of Company, Location of Policy, Insurance Agent

_____

_____

PENSIONS/ANNUITIES:

IF FEDERAL RETIREE: PIN NUMBER: _____

NAME OF SURVIVOR _____

SURVIVOR PIN NUMBER _____

BANK

Name and address of Bank, Account Number,
Location of Safe Deposit Box and Key

_____

_____

SECURITIES

Name and telephone number of broker

_____

TAX RECORDS FOR PAST 3 YEARS

LOCATION _____

Name and telephone number of accountant

_____

WHEN TO UPDATE YOUR ESTATE PLAN

We discussed people's natural disinclination to make an estate plan until they are faced with their own mortality. Many believe that they will make just one Will and then die (maybe that's why they put off making a Will). The reality is, most people who make a Will change it at least once before they die. If you have an estate plan, it is important to update it when any of the following events take place:

✍ A CHANGE IN RELATIONSHIP

You should examine your Estate Plan on a regular basis to determine whether it needs to be revised. If you decide that your Will needs revision, then it is important to have a new Will prepared. If you simply rip up the old Will, that will effectively revoke the Will (MCL 700.2507). But it could happen that someone (perhaps your attorney) has a copy of the Will. If no one knows that you revoked the Will, they may think the Will is lost and then offer the copy of the Will for Probate (see page 74). If you draft a new Will, then it should say, "I revoke all prior Wills ..."

BENEFICIARY MOVES OR DIES

Most people remember to name an alternate beneficiary should a beneficiary die during ones lifetime. But how many of us remember to notify the pension plan or insurance company of a change of address? It is important that your beneficiary's address be available to those in charge of distributing funds upon your death. Many insurance policies are never paid because the company cannot locate the beneficiary. In 1998, the Office of Federal Employees' Group Life Insurance reported that they had 29 million dollars in unpaid benefits, mostly because the beneficiary could not be located at their last given address.

CHANGE IN MARITAL STATUS

If your marry or divorce, there are certain changes that take place by law. For example, if you divorce and then die before you get around to changing your Will or trust, then any provision that you made for your ex-spouse in the document will be read as if your ex-spouse died before you (MCL 700.2807). But it is important to not just rely on the law. Best to change all documents after a divorce or separation. This includes deeds, Durable Power of Attorney, Patient Advocate Designation, insurance, etc.

NOTIFY EMPLOYER OF CHANGE IN RELATIONSHIP

If you change your marital status you need to tell your employer of the change so that the employer can change your status for purposes of paycheck withdrawals and health insurance coverage, and change of beneficiary for your Pension Plan.

RELOCATION TO A NEW STATE OR COUNTRY

There is no need to change your Estate Plan for a move within state. If you changed your county of residence and you deposited your original Will with the Clerk of the Probate Court, then you need to retrieve that Will and deposit it with the Register in the county of your new residence. Similarly, if you move to a new state, then you need to retrieve your Will from the Clerk and take it with you to the new state. Not every state allows the deposit of a Will prior to the death of the Will maker. You may need to make other arrangements to store your Will in the new state.

If you move to another state or country, it is important to either educate yourself about the laws of the state, or to consult with an attorney who can assist you in reviewing your estate plan to see if that plan will accomplish your goals in that state.

There is much to check out for a move to another state or country. Each state (and country) has its own laws relating to the inheritance of property and those laws are very different from each other. The rights of a spouse to inherit property varies significantly from state to state. If you have a Will or Trust, and you are married, then you need to check with an attorney to be sure that your Will or Trust cannot be challenged by your spouse because it does not conform to the laws of the state.

You also need to check out the taxes of the new state. Each state has its own estate tax structure. Some states have an inheritance tax, or a transfer tax on all inherited property. If state taxes are high, you may need an Estate Plan that will minimize the impact of those taxes. Creditor protection is another item that is significantly different state to state. If you have much debt, then determine what items can be inherited by your family free of your debts.

Each state has its own, unique, laws of Intestate Succession. Who has the right to inherit your property in Michigan may be different from who can inherit your property in another state. If you do not have a Will, then this is the time to think about who will get your property in the state of your residence. If you have a Will, Patient Advocate Designation or Power of Attorney, then you need to determine whether these documents will be honored in the new state. Laws relating to health care vary significantly. Other states may not have Patient Advocates, but they may have laws that enable you to appoint a Health Care Surrogate or a Health Care Agent with the right to make your health care decisions in the event that you are too ill to do so yourself. It is best to sign a new health care document using the form that is recognized in that state, rather than chance any confusion should you become ill and find yourself in an emergency situation.

✍ A SIGNIFICANT CHANGE IN THE LAW

We pay our legislators (state and federal) to make laws and, if necessary, change those in effect. We pay judges to interpret the law and that interpretation may change the way the law operates. The legislature and the judiciary do their job and so laws change frequently. Tax laws are particularly volatile. The 2001 change in the tax law not only changed income taxes, it significantly increased the Exclusion amount so that by 2010 no Estate Tax will be due regardless of the value of your Estate. You may be thinking that there is no need for an Estate Tax plan because you don't intend to die prior to 2010. But any certainty relating to death and taxes is false security (especially taxes, in this case). As explained in Chapter 8, the law as passed in 2001, is effective only until December 31, 2010. If lawmakers do nothing, then in 2011, the Federal Estate Tax goes back into effect; and estates that exceed one million dollars will once again be subject to Estate taxes.

And that is not the only uncertainty. Each state has its own Estate Tax structure. It remains to be seen how each state will react to the Federal change. Some states may follow the lead of the Federal government and increase their Estate Tax exemption in the same manner. Other states may see this as an opportunity to "pick up the slack" i.e., to increase their Estate Taxes, so that monies that would have been paid to the Federal government will now be paid to the state.

You need to keep up with the news to learn about changes in the law that affect your estate plan. It is a good idea to check with your attorney on a regular basis to see if any change in the state or Federal law affects your current Estate plan. Also check out the Eagle Publishing Company Web site for changes we will post to keep this book fresh:
http://www.eaglepublishing.com

GAMES DECEDENTS PLAY

We discussed the game of "hide and seek" some decedents play with their heirs. A variation of that game is the "wild goose chase." The person who plays this game is one who never updates his files. His records are filled with all sorts of lapsed insurance policies, promissory notes of debts long since paid; brokerage statements of securities that have been sold, and so on.

When he is gone, his family will become frustrated as they try to hunt down the "missing" asset. If you wish to play this game, then the best joke is to keep the key to a safe deposit box that you are no longer leasing. That will keep folks hunting for a long time!

If you do not have a wicked sense of humor, then do your family a favor and update your records on a regular basis.

Glossary

ADMINISTRATION The *administration* of a Probate Estate is the management and settlement of the decedent's affairs. There are different types of administration. See *Ancillary Administration* and *Summary administration.*

AFFIANT An *affiant* is someone who signs an affidavit and swears that it is true in the presence of a Notary Public or other person with authority to administer an oath.

AFFIDAVIT An *affidavit* is a written statement of fact made by someone voluntarily and under oath, in the presence of a notary public or someone else who has authority to administer an oath.

AGENT An *agent* is someone who is authorized by another (the principal) to act for or in place of the principal.

ANATOMICAL GIFT An *anatomical gift* is the donation of all or part of the body of the decedent for a specified purpose, such as transplantation or research.

ANCILLARY ADMINISTRATION An *ancillary administration* is a probate procedure that aids or assists the original (primary) probate proceeding. Ancillary administration is conducted in another state to determine the beneficiary of the decedent's property located within that state, and to determine whether the property is taxable in that state.

ANNUITANT An *annuitant* is someone who is entitled to receive payments under an annuity contract.

ANNUITY An *annuity* is a contract that gives someone (the annuitant) the right to receive periodic payments (monthly, quarterly) either for life or for a number of years.

ASSET An *asset* is anything owned by someone that has a value, including personal property (jewelry, paintings, securities, cash, motor vehicles, etc.) and real property (condominiums, vacant lots, acreage, residences, etc.)

ATTESTING WITNESS An *attesting witness* to a Will is someone who signs the Will, at the request of the person making the Will, in the presence of the person making the Will, for the purpose of proving that the Will maker signed the Will and did so of his own free will.

BENEFICIARY A *beneficiary* is one who benefits from the act of another or from the transfer of property. Examples include someone named in a Will or Trust to receive property, or someone who inherits property under the Laws of Intestate Succession.

CAVEAT *Caveat* is Latin for "Let him beware." It is a warning for the reader to be careful.

CHARITABLE REMAINDER ANNUITY TRUST   A *Charitable Remainder Annuity Trust* is a Trust that is required to pay an annuity to a designated person for a certain period of time. Once the annuity is paid, whatever remains in the Trust is donated to a tax exempt charity.

CLAIM A *Claim* against the decedent's estate is a demand for payment. To be effective, the claim must be filed with the Probate court within the time limits set by law.

CODE A *Code* is a body of laws arranged systematically for easy reference e.g. the Internal Revenue Code.

CODICIL A *Codicil* to a Will is supplement or an addition to a Will that changes certain parts of the Will.

COLUMBARIUM A *Columbarium* is a vault with niches (spaces) for urns that contain the ashes of cremated bodies.

COMMON LAW MARRIAGE A *Common Law marriage* is one that is entered into without a state marriage license nor any kind of official marriage ceremony. A common law marriage is created by an agreement to marry, followed by the two living together as man and wife. Most states do not recognize a common law marriage.

CONSERVATOR A *Conservator* is someone appointed by the Court to manage the property of a person who is unable to do so himself.

COURT The *Court* as used in this book is the Probate Court. When referring to an order made by the court then the term is synonymous with "judge," i.e., an "order of the court" is an order made by the judge of the court.

CREMAINS The word *Cremains* is an abbreviation of the term *cremated remains*. It is also referred to as the *ashes* of a person who has been cremated.

CURTESY *Curtesy* is the right of a husband, upon the death of his wife, to a life estate in real property she owned during their marriage, provided they had a surviving child who could inherit the property. Michigan abolished this English Common Law, but not Dower rights (the corresponding right for a woman).

DECEDENT The *Decedent* is the person who died.

DISTRIBUTION The *distribution* of a Trust estate or of a Probate Estate is the transfer to a beneficiary that part of the estate to which the beneficiary is entitled.

D.I.Y. DO-IT-YOURSELF.

DOWER *Dower* is the right of a wife to a life estate in 1/3rd of all property owned by her husband at any time during the course of their marriage. This Michigan law is based on the English Common Law. Most other states have abolished the law.

DURABLE POWER OF ATTORNEY A *Durable Power of Attorney* is a document in which a person (the *Principal*) gives another person (his *Agent* or *Attorney in Fact*) authority to do certain things on behalf of the Principal. The word *"durable"* means that the authority of the Agent continues even if the Principal is incapacitated at the time that the Agent is acting on behalf of the Principal.

ESTATE A person's *Estate* is all of the property (both real and personal property) owned by that person. A person's estate is also referred to as his *Taxable Estate* because all of the decedent's assets must be included when determining whether any Estate taxes are due when the person dies. Compare to Probate Estate.

EXECUTOR An *Executor* is someone appointed by a Will maker to carry out the directions and requests in his Will.

ET SEQ. *Et seq.* is an abbreviation for *et sequentia* which is Latin for "and the following." A reference to statute 490.1 et seq. is a reference to the remaining statutes in that section of the Michigan Code i.e., 490.2, 490.3, . . .

FIDUCIARY A *Fiduciary* is one who holds property in trust for another or one who acts for the benefit of another. This term includes a Personal Representative, trustee, guardian, conservator, etc.

GRANTEE the *Grantee* (also called the party of the second part) named in a deed is the person who receives title to the property from the grantor.

GRANTOR A *Grantor* is someone who transfers property. The grantor of a deed is the person who transfers property to a new owner (the *Grantee*). The grantor of a trust is someone who creates the trust and then transfer's property into the trust.

GUARDIAN A *Guardian* is someone who has legal authority to care for the person or property of a minor or for the person of someone who has been found by the court to be incapacitated.

HEIR An *Heir* is someone who is entitled to inherit the decedent's property in the event that the decedent dies without a Will.

HOMESTEAD The *homestead* is the dwelling and land owned and occupied as the owner's principal residence.

INCAPACITATED The term *incapacitated* is used in two ways. A person is *physically incapacitated* if he lacks the ability to care for himself in some way. A person is *legally incapacitated* if a court finds that a person is unable to care for his person or property. Once the Court determines that a person is legally incapacitated, the judge will appoint someone to care for person or property of the incapacitated person.

INDIGENT An person who is *indigent* is one who is poor, and without funds.

INTESTATE *Intestate* means not having a Will or dying without a Will. *Testate* is to have a Will or dying with a Will.

IRREVOCABLE CONTRACT An *irrevocable contract* is a contract that cannot be revoked, withdrawn, or cancelled by any of the parties to that contract.

JOINT AND SEVERAL LIABILITY   If two or more people agree to be *jointly and severally liable* to pay the debt, then that means that each individually agree to be responsible to pay the debt, and together they all agree to pay for the debt.

KEY MAN INSURANCE   *Key man insurance* is an insurance policy designed to protect a company from economic loss in the event that an important employee of the company becomes disabled or dies.

LEGALESE   *Legalese* refers to the use of legal terms and confusing text that is used by many attorneys to draft legal documents.

LETTERS OF AUTHORITY   *Letters of Authority* is a document, issued by the Probate court, giving the Personal Representative authority to take possession of and to administer the estate of the decedent.

LIEN   A *Lien* is a charge against a person's property as security for a debt. The lien is evidence of the creditor's right to take the property as full or partial payment, in the event that the debtor defaults in paying the monies owed.

LIFE ESTATE A *Life Estate* interest in real property is the right to possess and occupy that property for so long as the holder of the life estate lives.

LINEAL DESCENDANT A *Lineal Descendant* of the decedent is someone who is his direct descendant, such as his child, grandchild, great-grandchild etc.

LITIGATION   *Litigation* is the process of carrying on a lawsuit, i.e., to sue for some right or remedy in a court of law. A Litigation Attorney is one who is experienced in conducting the law suit and in particular, going to trial.

LIVING WILL   A *Living Will* is a document that gives instructions about whether life support systems should be withheld in the event that the person who signs the Living Will is terminally ill or in a persistent vegetative state and unable to speak for himself.

MEDICAID *Medicaid* is a public assistance program sponsored jointly by the federal and state government to provide medical care for people with low income.

NET PROCEEDS The *Net Proceeds* of a sale is the sales price less costs incurred to make that sale.

NET WORTH A person's *Net Worth* is the value of all of the property that he owns less the monies owed on that property.

NEXT OF KIN   *Next of kin* has two meanings in law: *next of kin* can refer to a person's nearest blood relation or it can refer to those people (not necessarily blood relations) who are entitled to inherit the property of the decedent if the decedent died without a will.

PATIENT ADVOCATE DESIGNATION   In   Michigan, a *Patient Advocate Designation* is a document signed by someone (the Patient) appointing another (his Advocate) to make health care decisions in the event the Patient is too ill to do so himself. In other states a Patient Advocate is referred to as a *Health Care Agent* or a *Health Care Surrogate*.

PERJURY *Perjury* is lying under oath. The false statement can be made as a witness in court or by signing an Affidavit. Perjury is a criminal offense.

PERSONAL PROPERTY *Personal property* is all property owned by a person that is not real property (real estate). It includes cars, stocks, house furnishings, jewelry, etc.

PERSONAL REPRESENTATIVE A *Personal Representative* is someone who is appointed by the Probate court to settle the decedent's estate and to distribute whatever is left to the proper beneficiary.

PER STIRPES GIFT A *Per Stirpes* gift is a gift which is given to a group of people such that if one of them dies before the gift is given, then that deceased person's share goes to his/her lineal descendants.

PETITION A *Petition* is a formal written request to a Court asking the Court to take action or issue an order on a given matter.

POST-NUPTIAL AGREEMENT A *Post-nuptial agreement* is an agreement made by a couple after marriage to decide their respective rights in case of a dissolution or the death of a spouse

POWER OF ATTORNEY A *Power of Attorney* is a document in which the person who signs the document (the *Principal*) gives another person (his *Agent*) authority to do certain things on behalf of the Principal.

PRE-NUPTIAL AGREEMENT A *Pre-nuptial agreement* (also known as an *Antenuptial agreement*) is an agreement made prior to marriage whereby a couple determines how their property is to be managed during their marriage and how their property is to be divided should one die, or they later divorce.

PROBATE   *Probate* is a court procedure in which a court determines the existence of a valid Will and then supervises the distribution of the Probate Estate of the decedent.

PROBATE ESTATE   The *Probate Estate* is that part of the decedent's estate that is subject to probate. It includes property that the decedent owned in his name only. It does not include property that was jointly held by the decedent and someone else. It does not include property held "in trust for" or "for the benefit of" someone.

REAL PROPERTY   *Real property,* also known as *real estate,* is land and anything permanently attached to the land such as buildings and fences.

RESIDENT AGENT A *Resident Agent* of a Michigan corporation is someone who is authorized to act on behalf of the company and accept service of process in the event the company is sued.

RESIDUARY BENEFICIARY   A *residuary beneficiary* is a beneficiary named in a Will who is to receive all or part of whatever is left of the Probate Estate once the specific gifts made in the Will have been distributed and once the decedent's bills, taxes and costs of probate have been paid.

RESIDUARY ESTATE   A *Residuary Estate* is that part of a
        probate estate that is left after all expenses and costs of
        administration have been paid and specific gifts have
        been distributed.

SELF-PROVED WILL   A *Self-proved Will* is a Will that has a
        section stating two witnesses to the Will verify that the
        Will maker was over 18 and signed the Will voluntarily
        and that the Will maker and the witnesses signed the
        document in the presence of a Notary Public. Michigan
        statute 700.2504 has a statutory form of a Self-Proof
        provision. Once the Will is Self-proved, it can be
        admitted to Probate without the need for the witnesses
        to testify to the above facts.

SETTLOR   A *Settlor* is someone who furnishes property that is
        placed in a trust. If the Settlor is also the creator of the
        trust, then the Settlor is also referred to as the Grantor.

SPENDTHRIFT   A *Spendthrift* is someone who spends money
        carelessly or wastefully or extravagantly.

SPENDTHRIFT TRUST   A *Spendthrift Trust* is a trust created to
        provide monies for the living expenses of a beneficiary,
        and at the same time protect the monies from being
        taken by the creditors of the beneficiary.

STATUTE OF LIMITATION A *Statute of Limitation* is a federal or
        state law that sets maximum time periods for taking
        legal action. Once the time set out in the statute passes,
        no legal action can be taken.

TENANCY BY THE ENTIRETY   A *Tenancy by the Entirety* is the
        name of a form of ownership of real property held by a
        husband and wife. It has the same legal effect as a
        joint tenancy with right of survivorship.

It is the goal of EAGLE PUBLISHING COMPANY to keep our publications fresh.

We posted an update to this edition at our Web site:
    http://www.eaglepublishing.com

The update explains the recent change in the Estate Tax law.

If you do not have Internet access, call us at
    (800) 824-0823
and we will mail the update to you.

TENANCY IN COMMON *Tenancy in common* is a form of ownership such that each Tenant owns his/her share without any claim to that share by the other Tenants. There is no right of survivorship. Once a Tenant In Common dies, his/her share belongs to the Tenant's estate and not to the remaining owners.

TESTATE *Testate* means having a Will or dying with a Will.

TITLE INSURANCE *Title Insurance* is a policy issued by a title company after searching title to the property. The policy insures the accuracy of its search against any claim of a defective title.

TRUST A *Trust* is a legal document in which someone (the Grantor) appoints a trustee to manage property placed into the trust. The purpose of the trust is to benefit persons or charities named by the Grantor as beneficiaries of the trust.

TRUSTEE A *Trustee* is a person, or institution, who accepts the duty of caring for property for the benefit of another.

UNDUE INFLUENCE *Undue influence* is pressure, influence or persuasion that overpowers a person's free will or judgment, so that a person acts according to the will or purpose of the dominating party.

WAIVER A *waiver* is the intentional and voluntary giving up of a known right.

WARRANTY DEED A *warranty deed* is a deed in which someone (the Grantor) transfers the property to another (the Grantee) and guarantees good title, i.e., the Grantor guarantees that he has the right to transfer the property, and that no one else has any right to the property.

WRONGFUL DEATH   A *wrongful death* is a death that was caused by the willful or negligent act of a person or company.

INDEX

A

B

M

MAIL   59

MARRIAGE
  Common Law   110
  Same Sex   110

MARRIED WOMAN'S RTS   78

MEDICAID   17, 82, 162
                    184, 245, 246

MEDICAL EXAMINER   3, 18, 20

MEDICARE   47
  Appeal   87
  Billing   86
  Coverage   87, 243
  Fraud   85
  Hotline   85
  Payments   82
  Spouse's Coverage   48

MICHIGAN
  Agency (see STATE AGENCY)
  Statutes (see STATUTES)

MILITARY BURIAL
        15-17, 157, 254

MINOR CHILD   89, 118, 139, 177
         183, 202, 208-213

MISSING BODY   22

MOBILE HOME   134

MORTGAGE INSUR.   46, 222

MOTOR VEHICLE
  Gift   200
  Held in Trust   107
  Insurance   41, 100
  Jointly Held   100
  Leased   63, 135, 221, 222
  Lost Title   63
  Transfer   131-133
  Value of   132

N

NEGLECTFUL PARENT   119

NET WORTH   234, 235, 249

NEXT OF KIN   22, 27, 59
             100, 102, 112

NON MARITAL CHILD   116

NOTARY PUBLIC   203

NURSING HOME   80, 81

O

OFFICE OF PERSONNEL
  MANAGEMENT   30, 244

ORGAN PROCUREMENT
  ORGANIZATION   4, 5

OUT OF STATE
  Account   67
  Burial   14
  Deed   106
  Property   106, 142, 187
  Residence   74
  Will   73

OVERWEIGHT, decedent   12

184 Michigan Statutes are referenced in
Guiding Those Left Behind In Michigan

Each state has its own set of laws relating to the settlement of a person's estate. The Michigan laws that are referenced in this book are very different from the laws of other states. The author is in now in the process of "translating" *Guiding Those Left Behind . . .* for the rest of the states; that is, to write a book that incorporates the laws of the state into a book that describes how to settle the affairs of a decedent in that state, and how to prepare an estate plan that is appropriate for the state.

Arizona, California, Florida, Georgia, Indiana, Illinois, Maryland, Massachusetts, Michigan, New Jersey, New York, North Carolina, Ohio, Pennsylvania, Tennessee, Texas, Virginia, Wisconsin and Washington are now in print.

The following books are scheduled for release by January, 2002:
> *Guiding Those Left Behind In Alabama*
> *Guiding Those Left Behind In Colorado*
> *Guiding Those Left Behind In South Carolina*
> *Guiding Those Left Behind In Minnesota*
> *Guiding Those Left Behind In Missouri*

To order a book call **(800) 824-0823.**
Visit our Web site **http://www.eaglepublishing.com**
to check whether books for other states are available at
this time.

BOOK REVIEWS FROM DIFFERENT STATES

ARIZONA

Ben T. Traywick of the Tombstone Epitaph said "This book is an excellent reference book that simplifies all the necessary tasks that must be done when there is a death in the family. There is even an explanation as to how you can arrange your own estate so that your heirs will not be left with a multitude of nagging problems." "The reviewer has been going through probate for two years with no end yet in sight. This book at the beginning two year ago would have helped immensely."

CALIFORNIA

Margot Petit Nichols of the Carmel Pine Cone called it a ". . .TRULY RIVETING READ." " . . . I could scarcely put it down." "This is a book that we should all have, either on our book shelves or thoughtfully placed with our important papers."

FLORIDA

Maryhelen Clague of the Tampa Tribune Times wrote "Amelia Pohl has created a handy, self-help guide that illustrates the necessary steps that must be taken when someone dies, a guide that is easy to read, extremely clear and simple to refer to when the need arises."

NEW YORK

Saul Friedman of NEWSDAY said "And one section that should be read by readers of any age, suggests and describes how to create an 'If I Die' file to point the way to your vital papers and policies, to minimize the problems and costs for your survivors. Alas, not even you boomers will live forever."

AMELIA E. POHL and the noted psychologist BARBARA J. SIMMONDS, Ph.d, have written a book for those families who have suffered a loss.

Beyond Grief To Acceptance and Peace explains:
- ✧ What to say to the bereaved
- ✧ How to help a child through the loss
- ✧ Strategies to adjust to a new life style
- ✧ When and where to seek assistance.

The second edition of this 80 page book is now available for $9.95 plus shipping and handling. You can order the book using the following discount coupon for a total of $9.

DISCOUNT COUPON

Please send me a copy of Beyond Grief To Acceptance and Peace

☐ I am enclosing a check for $9.
☐ Charge this to my _____ credit card
(Visa, Master, etc.)

Credit Card no. _____

Expiration date: _____

Name _____

Address _____

_____

Mail this coupon to:
EAGLE PUBLISHING COMPANY OF BOCA
4199 N. Dixie Hwy. #2
Boca Raton, FL 33431